La Bella
Cucina

LA BELLA CUCINA

Traditional Recipes from a Sicilian Kitchen

MIMMETTA LO MONTE

BEAUFORT BOOKS, INC.
New York / Toronto

Contents

Library of Congress Cataloging in Publication Data

Lo Monte, Mimmetta.
La bella cucina.

Includes index.
1. Cookery, Italian.   2. Sicily—Social life and customs.   I. Title.
TX723.L57   1983   641.945'8   83-7112
ISBN 0-8253-0149-1

Published in the United States by Beaufort Books,
Inc., New York. Published simultaneously in Canada by
General Publishing Co. Limited

Designer: Ellen LoGiudice

Printed in the U.S.A.   First Edition

10   9   8   7   6   5   4   3   2   1

Acknowledgements

To the Siragusa family: for safekeeping the culinary tradition passed on to me.

To my daughter, my husband, my friends, and my students: for their support and encouragement while testing and tasting my recipes.

To Betsy Mirel: for first giving me the idea of writing a cookbook.

To William Rice: for his professional acceptance and recognition of my cooking.

To my father

Foreword

Italians seem to have quite a number of mottos; said to represent the wisdom of the people, they are often quoted and seldom followed. But there is one that is quoted by the entire population of Italy, regardless of age, sex, or status: "*A tavola non si invecchia,*" that is, "at the dining table one doesn't get any older."

The time taken sitting at the table and eating is not wasted time. Enjoy your meal at your leisure, and enjoy, too, all the other pleasures to be found around the table: conversing, maintaining strong ties with the family, renewing old friendships. Some meals have deep cultural undertones: traditions have been renewed for centuries at the table as have religions at the altar. Birthdays, weddings, anniversaries, and holidays are identified with particular meals.

Italians are basically sensuous: they translate impalpable and spiritual events, such as "L'Assunzione della Vergine," or national holidays, such as "La Liberazione," into feasts without being blasphemous or disrespectful. In fact it is to honor the Virgin and the country that they get together and celebrate with a good amount of food, friends, and relatives.

I learned to love food in Sicily, where I was born. Sicily is the largest island in the Mediterranean. Triangular in shape, the island has been represented from the most ancient times by the symbol of a face around which three legs extend symmetrically. The Greeks named it Trinacria which means "three capes."

9

There are many ways to discover the variety of people who, through the centuries, have conquered, ruled, respected, or abused this land, as they have left a mark in the race, in the monuments, in the vegetation, and in the food. To talk of food, forgetting the people, their culture, and their environment, would deprive the food of its most important components, as they all interrelate very closely. Many foods are tied to images in my mind: a shepherd, covered to his eyebrows with a rough wool hat and wrapped in the typical cape worn in the fields, stirring a huge pot in the courtyard, as he is watched carefully by children. We children are ready to extend our cupped hands to receive a scoop of whey he offers us. Or the image of my mother and one of her brothers arguing about how much corn-starch to put in the "gelo di melone," an argument that started when I was a small child and is still going on today. Or the worried expression of my mother watching my brother when-ever he came home on a brief vacation from medical school as he brought to his mouth a bite of carefully prepared food and slowly chewed it. Her face relaxed as he approved and gave his favorable opinion. (Sometimes her expression was one of dis-may when he started his criticism—while stuffing himself in the meantime.)

There are some respected family authorities who are always consulted whenever there is going to be a big dinner or a special event. My mother is the uncontested oracle, but when her father, Nonno Alfredo, was alive, he was the gourmet and expert.

I spent a lot of time during my childhood with both my paternal and maternal grandparents, and this exposed me to two entirely different ways of perceiving both food and life.

The pictures of my paternal grandparents, Nonno Giovanni and Nonna Adelina, stare at me from my desk: he, a young man with a half-humorous dandyish expression; she, a girl with a head full of hair and a slender waist—the photographer captured the boldness of her youth in sharp contrast with a very romantic setting. Nonno was always very active and very busy, but his activities were never taken leisurely. He would take the time to listen to me and be amused but was a little worried by the rebellion he probably could detect in me. Nonna Adelina, a very strong-minded woman, who held the keys to his heart, his bank deposit box, and to the pantry, was also very parsimonious and very careful that nothing would go to waste, including her time and her feelings. Meals at her home reflected her personality.

The huge table saw foods that were produced from the farms. Meats were often lamb, kid, or chicken (heads and guts included, stripped of any offending taste by energetic scrubbing and blanching, and prepared in very palatable fashion).

The first course was invariably pasta, which was combined with plain tomato sauce from bottles prepared by the women in one of the farms during the summer, or with the juice of the cooked meats, chicken broth, or very simply with fresh, pungent olive oil just out of the press. Grated *caciocavallo* or *pecorino* worked wonders sprinkled on top of the pasta, regardless of the sauce. The food was without any fuss: wholesome and almost entirely self-produced. The lack of variety in everyday food was made up by the frequent change in pasta shapes. The family Nonna came from held the monopoly on the pasta industry in western Sicily and owned a good-size produce canning-plant. You can imagine why there was no end to the supply or variety of pasta—(I never saw rice on her table)—or tomato sauce. If the supply of the homemade sauce ran low, there were stacks of canned peeled tomatoes waiting to be opened.

Some of the members of the family have since shifted their interest from flour and food processing to more intellectual activities, such as teaching or practicing law or medicine, and probably can't even distinguish wheat from oats any more. Others, however, have hung onto the family tradition (and money) and still produce pasta.

When there was a special occasion, like her saint's day, or Nonno's, then food was a different matter to my grandmother. The pasta *ncaciata* overflowing with cheese and *ragù*, which is made by simmering meats and/or vegetables, made its appearance as did squabs, sausage, roasted potatoes, and plenty of any vegetable in season—both cooked and raw. (Very shrewdly she had married off one of her daughters to a man who had sizeable cultivations of peaches, pears and artichokes, therefore supplying the family with items they didn't produce.)

Fresh ricotta and other cheeses followed the main course. The meal was accompanied by wine from the farm and topped off with a small cup of thick black coffee (of which I was allowed just a sip) and pastries and fruit. Just as everyone had been rushing to get this meal started and served, now they rushed to repair the consequences of it. My mother would run into the kitchen and prepare some hot water with a bay leaf for my father, watching him as he sipped from the steaming cup while walking back and forth, waiting for the miraculous potion to settle his stomach.

Nonna would accompany Nonno to his armchair, remove his glasses, and gently lay a bouclé shawl on his legs. Then hand-in-hand with Nonna, we walked to our treat: the daybed where we cuddled together. I whispered to her for a while, making up stories, and then she would fall asleep but I never did. I just waited very quietly, careful not to move and disturb her rest, enjoying this intimacy that I knew was very special since none of her other grandchildren was offered this privilege nor were any of her children. As a young woman she had chosen to be at her husband's side rather than occupy herself with child care and chores. She delegated the responsibility for the boy to a nurse and for the girls to a convent school.

Now she lavished on me all the affection she hadn't expressed earlier. And as I grew older, while circumstances and lifestyles changed, the closeness of those days still stayed intact. Today, during the brief periods I spend in Palermo, I'll visit her, an old woman alone with her maid in a big house, and she'll always have a treat for me. She always got the ingredients out of the riposto, a storage room for food, herself, me at her heels, waiting for the door to open. On the other side was a small, cool room where I'd inhale the pungent smell of cheese and take in the heavenly vision of food: lined up on the shelves were the bottled tomato sauce, braids of garlic and of onions; dried sausage and dried figs were strung through cane sticks or yucca ropes and hanging from hooks. And below them the tin cans containing *buccellatini*, Sicilian Christmas dessert, guava chunks, and almond pastries, on which my eyes concentrated with expectation until I saw her take a can and remove from it a treat that she would offer with a few words of warning: "Now, be sure that after this you can still eat your dinner." Off I went to the garden, nibbling on my sweet treasure.

I peeked through the iron fence to the people in the street and then walked along the paved paths, studying the aphids in the roses and picking jasmine, which I gathered in my skirt by holding the hem up. Then a clear feminine voice would break through the garden, calling, "*E'pronto!*," putting an end to my wait. I'd run in and dump my collection of white blossoms in a green glass bowl and the subtle scent would soon fill the room. A quick trip to wash my hands and then I sat on my chair at the dining room table and feasted on minestrone, big chunks of fried potatoes, and *bianco mangiare* (white pudding) with marsala-soaked biscuits.

I remember the trips to Cannavata, the closest family farm and the one that offered the most comforts. To me these trips seemed interminable, submerged in the backseat of the car next to my grandparents. Andrea, the chauffeur, drove solidly and evenly, his hawklike face concentrated on the road, squinting his eyes in the bright light created by the sun and the yellow reflection of the fields gilded with ripe wheat. Poor Andrea, he didn't know that some of his trouble adjusting to that unmerciful light dated to many centuries before, when northern men who endowed Sicily with marvelous monuments also bequeathed pale green eyes like his that are very unsuitable in a sunbeaten land.

The road wound up and through Marineo, a village perenially threatened by landslides and the town closest to the farm. The central square was the place of a ritual stop where obsequious men came to the windows, to greet the *onorevole*, "most honorable" and "La Signora Adelina." Grandmother, fanning herself with quick movements of the black fan that constantly hung from her neck by a thin silk cord, asked very spare questions, and from the way the men were twisting in their hands the caps they had taken off at the sight of the car, I could tell when she was putting them on the spot.

Someone would always offer to buy an ice cream for my brother and me. We both happily licked our creamy lemon iced cones, *cono gelato*. Lemon was the only flavor we were allowed to accept, as it didn't contain any milk and from a hygienic standpoint was the safest in that heat.

The farm meant freedom to me. The land was there; the soft hills dipped into one another; the wind when it swept through the wheat made it alive, and the birds rose suddenly, small shapes against the sky. The spot of green of the vineyard, the eucalypti embracing the sloping side of the hill where the house stood, and the sun pouring its light from the most incredibly blue sky I have ever seen made an indelible impression. From the excitement of picking the fruit and the vegetables we would later eat, I went to the thrill of chasing away the chickens from their nests to get the eggs, still warm. I, who was the smallest and stayed so, was the one sent up to the *piccionaia*, the pigeon house. A long climb on a wooden ladder to the tiniest door, a struggle with the big iron key, and then after a few seconds of adjustment to the darkness, I saw the light break through and touch the squabs.

I crawled on my hands and knees in the straw, avoiding carefully the small eggs in it. Then I would select the birds that had some feathers on (but not enough feathers to fly away through the triangular openings, as the adults had already done when I had fumbled with the key).

There was one room, off the main stable, where the kids were kept in the dark and milk fed. There was a great difference in the flavor of their meat and that of the ones who were allowed to graze. They were kept as a delicacy, to be slaughtered for special events. At dusk the smell of burning wood from the open fires of the shepherds, busily coagulating the milk collected during the day to transform it into cheese, mingled with the smell of lamb roasting on the wood coals. The chill of the night found us tired, ready to enjoy a thick slice of sourdough bread and a piece of *tuma*, "fresh unprocessed cheese." The meat was accompanied by a substantial salad of tomatoes, onions, and olives, exuding a strong smell of vinegar. The salad was followed by a bowl of fruit we had picked: figs, mulberries —huge and juicy—or grapes. Along with the fruit we had raw vegetables, fava beans, fennel, radishes. Fresh fruit and vegetables appeared according to the season, but there were always plenty of dried figs, walnuts, and almonds. Everybody would peel fruit and share it, and we would, in turn, prepare figs stuffed with almonds or walnuts and offer them with affection.

We often sat together—grandmother, mother, maids, and farm women—and shelled fava beans and peas or fresh beans, a basketful of them in the middle, the older women gathering them in their calico aprons, while I was given a small bowl to fill on my lap. We chatted. I was always asked by my grandmother to recite poems I learned in school, and I did, half-choking since I was very shy. I was rewarded in the end by a chorus of "che sapurita," which means pretty. This made me wiggle in my seat, extending my blushing to my ears, and made me wish I was a boy so that I could make the rounds with my grandfather to check over the workers, the machinery, the wheat being harvested and weighed in, and the payroll.

At one time I did pretend to be a boy. I took a toy rifle and tumbled down a flight of steps with it. I found myself at the feet of several adults, who, after making sure that I hadn't suffered any damage except a few bruises and bumps, lectured me. They took the gun away, gave it back to my brother, and left me convinced that the whole system was very unfair but hard to beat. For the time being I abandoned my fantasies of adventures and resigned myself to sit on my midget-size chair and shell beans.

Looking back, I can't say that I regret my decision; I was to realize very soon that the world of women was a mystery to men. They never took the time to discover it, while their world was an open book to me since I had not given up observation. I also sensed that this circle of chatting women held the real power: the control of the table that was the point of encounter and the center of everyday life. Every activity began and ended there. The men didn't consider the work of the women as inferior to their own but rather as parallel. As time went on my visits to the farm were less frequent, but the special feeling of community and work that I acquired there stayed with me, as did recognition of different tasks and the acceptance of them as both being indispensable to the life of the family.

Donna Peppina had lived with the family, it seemed, forever. She came from a village that had a very strong ethnic character. It was a settlement of Albanians, who had maintained their language and their traditions. She never abandoned wearing the traditional clothes from her village, and as she walked around the house she seemed to float in her long dark skirt with a shawl draped around her shoulders.

She had reared my father, whom she called Cicciuzzu, since the age of two—had fed him and dressed him, had cuddled him and scolded him. She was the last person he'd see at night, and the first he'd see in the morning.

Cicciuzzu grew to be "Il Signorino" and too big for the material care she had provided. He eventually got married and had his own children, but he was never too old for her affection.

After more than twenty years of being part of the household, she had become indispensable to its smooth operation. She was the middle person between grandmother and the people who worked for her and made sure that grandmother's wishes were carried out. Donna Peppina was illiterate, but she had a great sense of propriety and dignity, and was blessed with an excellent memory.

The house had always streamed with people—farm workers, villagers, political friends, family friends, relatives,—who had come to see either one or both of my grandparents.

Warned by our chauffeur Andrea, who was also the guardian opening the gate for visitors, she screened them and directed them to the grand staircase that led to the main entrance hall, or up through the portico stairs to the everyday entrance.

Once in the house Donna Peppina juggled the guests according to rank and circumstances. Some were seated in the parlor, some in the drawing room. Others were directed to the family room, the den, or the study. Still others were stopped in the everyday entrance and sent to the kitchen.

Most of the food supplies were brought in by the farm workers and villagers. Donna Peppina examined and smelled the chickens, the lambs, the kids, the sausage, the slices of pork and the *castrato*, or "mutton"; she scrubbed the animals' stomach cavities with salt and saw that the innards were cooked at once. She methodically went through each crate of fruit and vegetables and each basket of eggs. Vegetables and fruit were selected according to their degree of ripeness and tenderness. They were either spread out or put together in bundles, some ready for immediate consumption; some to be saved.

Fruit past its peak was put aside to make jam, and excess ripe tomatoes were converted into sauce to be bottled and preserved. Cheese and milk were brought in all year, but in the summer months the milk production and its taste was affected by the herds feeding on dried-out pastures. The ricotta was silky smooth and rich, the milk hard to pour from the bottles—as a thick layer of cream had built up in the neck. Milk and ricotta refrigerated for more than two days were used for cooking. Milk was turned into *bianco mangiare* or some other kind of pudding, into béchamel sauce, and milk croquettes. Ricotta was fried, used for pasta dishes, and mixed with sugar to be used for desserts.

What I thought was most fun to watch was the egg selection. It was done in the kitchen at night. Donna Peppina, sitting at the huge table, lit a candle and switched off all the lights. The big pots and pans hanging around cast strange shadows on the walls; everything seemed bigger and unfamiliar, and I stuck to her as closely as possible. Her hands, brown and leathery, shook each egg gently near her ear, then held it in front of the flame. If okay, they went in a basket individually wrapped in pieces of paper.

The freshest eggs were eaten coddled, poached, and fried; the other eggs were used in *frittata* (eggs beaten together, with the addition of other ingredients such as cheese, herbs, vegetables, and fried), potato and rice dishes, and for general cooking.

Donna Peppina used all her senses to establish the quality of food. We may live in a different world and time from hers; but we do have the same senses, and we can put them to work to select better food whenever possible.

While at my paternal grandparents I was never surprised by the dishes that appeared on the table, and I learned to know and appreciate the food of the country in its simplicity, its flavor, and sometimes, its gaudiness. At my maternal grandparents and in my own home, I was in an atmosphere comparable to a glutton's paradise. My mother dished out delicacies, different every day, from first course to dessert.

Nonno Alfredo, opened my eyes to the secrets of gourmet cooking, and to the beautiful open markets in town. Found in the heart of the old Palermo, they unfold in narrow streets converging in a central piazza.

The food displays are magnificent, the shelves overflowing with vegetables and fruit. The fish, mixed with bright-green seaweed, is placed on a bed of crushed ice inside wooden boxes, and then neatly arranged on huge marble-top benches. The meats hang from powerful hooks. The butchers, towering from their elevated counters, have in front, as cutting blocks, tree sections on which they chop, pound, and cut. The loud voices of the fishmongers and fruitsellers, keep encouraging the shoppers to stop and buy their goods.

Nonno Alfredo did his shopping carefully, selecting price and quality with a trained eye. We would slowly fill up the shopping nets we both held. I bought myself smoked herring, which I later marinated in a sauce he had taught me to make from orange juice, lemon, olive oil, and pepper and served with orange slices. It was fit for a king's smorgasbord.

The vegetable stand offered gigantic baking trays filled with onions baked in their jackets and in blackened round-bellied copper pots, whole boiled-potatoes, and two-inch artichokes.

Pyramids of eggs, a miracle of white balance, rose under chickens hanging by their legs.

Fried chick-pea cakes, baby fish, cauliflower, fried eggplant —were hungrily eaten as a snack. For lunch these were stuffed in soft round breads. Prepared this way, the bread and vegetables are called *muffolette*. The trips to the market were exhausting, but what satisfaction we drew from the results! And when we got home, the kitchen became animated; the food was carefully washed and prepared so that the various dishes could take form.

Nonno was very efficient; food for him was art and chemistry. When he was through with a *caponata, pasta con sarde,* or cannoli, the eyes got as much satisfaction as the nose and the tastebuds. He was as much at ease fixing *spiedini* (skewered meat rolls or anything on skewers) as he was fixing a truffled dish or game. The tradition was passed on to him by his mother, who, in turn, had acquired this art from the chef who the family, at one time, was able to afford. The art now rested in safe hands, to be passed to his children and grandchildren.

All the elements of the meal—but one—were created by his hands. Indispensable complement to the meal, the bread was delivered by the bakery, crunchy fresh, at dinner and supper time.

What smell is more heartwarming than that of freshly baked bread? Coming to life in the hot ovens, it has not only the meaning of food tied to it but the meaning of nourishment necessary to life itself. Ceres, the goddess of Earth and fertility, was crowned by a wreath of wheat ears; bread is one of the oldest foods prepared by civilized men.

Bakeries in Palermo are the realization of the most refined and finicky, starch-loving choreographer: bread, honey-colored, encrusted with sesame seeds, or smooth and glowing, almost sensuous-looking. The bread awaits, still hot in huge baskets or, as it cools off, on shelves. Next to it all its derivatives: brioches, croissánts, *pâte feuilletée, sfincioni,* and cookies, fragrant with vanilla, cinnamon, and fennel seed.

The metamorphosis of shapes and sizes that bread undergoes might appear as the game of a bored baker; in fact it follows strict rules dictated by tradition.

Bread, to me, is the most normal answer to hunger. Eaten by itself, or with olives, cheese, or a tomato and onion salad flavored with oregano, bread becomes first course, second course, and—why not?—a most unusual dessert, eaten with grapes or walnuts, or stuffed with ice cream.

Bread levels the rich and the poor. Laid on a fine linen cloth, or on a rough table, hands will squeeze it in an almost uncon-scious movement to test the freshness. It will then be broken into bite-size pieces to accompany each mouthful of food, be the meal an expensive cut of meat or a simple soup.

Bread (*Grazia di Dio*) is considered a gift from God and, as such, no bread is allowed to go to waste. The bread not con-sumed during the day will become croutons, breadcrumbs, or a meal with bay leaves, pepper, grated cheese, olive oil, and water, or *pane cotto*.

As summer approached, we formulated plans to leave town to spend the hottest months in a cool place. Toward the end of school father and mother started worrying about how we had done with our studies. If we had failed any course, we would have to go to a place where we could be tutored.

Most of the time we ended up in Erice, a small village up at the top of a lonely mountain. It overlooked the sea at the extreme west point of Sicily. The village is very close to Trapani, a good-size town, to San Vito, an enchanting gold- and pink-colored beach strip, and to the Egadi Islands, three black sha-dows you can see from the belvedere of the Balio, the public garden of the village. Erice had served as a fortress and sanc-tuary for the Phoenicians, the Greeks, the Romans, and the Spaniards.

In that point of Sicily although only about one hundred kilo-meters from Palermo, exists a new world of colors, sounds, and shapes. People speak with high-pitched voices, in an almost singing fashion. They live in differently styled houses and eat a variety of foods. The rich pastures of the seas in the area, with their high salinity, give the fish a special flavor. Every morning fishmongers, driving scooters with small trailers loaded with fish, climb up the tortuous road that leads to the village. They either display in a minuscule fish market against the side wall of a church, or they scout through the narrow streets paved with white stones selling fish door to door.

We knew all of them, and we knew who brought which fish from where. Along the coast there were very distinct areas that had their specialties. Bonagia was famous for lobsters and the strange-shaped fish that was used for highly spiced soups that accompanied couscous. The Stagnone, a shallow, lagoonlike enclosure, supplied the finest white fish. And there was the fish brought in by the fleet of Mazara from the contended waters between Sicily and Tunisia.

Fish wasn't the only special item to be found in Erice. In two or three of the *caffè* or on or near the main piazza, you could find, made fresh every day, jasmine or cinnamon ice, and the nuns of the convent of San Carlo made delicious almond pastries and *mustazzoli*, very hard, huge cookies, spiced with cloves or sweetened with honey.

The village lived in its own dimension; often hidden by mist, surrounded by pines, it seemed to wake up in the summer, when vacationers like ourselves would search in its medieval charm for relief from the harassment and the noise of towns. I went often down a very narrow trail on expeditions to collect pine nuts. Spanish moss hung from the tree branches, making them look terribly ancient. Raising my head, I could see the ruins of the castle of Venere, clinging to the cliff, and the towers of the Castello Pepoli, and hear the voices of the children playing along the paths and the terraces of the Balio and the calls of their mothers. Once down the trail there was a clearing in the woods, surrounded by pine-nut-producing trees. The only noise was the crackling of the pine needles under my feet.

I made a pouch with my cotton scarf, and when it was full, I chose a good place to sit and with a couple of stones cracked some nuts. The fine brown powder from the shells coated my fingers and smeared my face and my clothes. The large pine umbrellas towered over the thorniest and most intricate blackberry bushes I have ever seen. The sunshine jewelled them in all shades of red. I ate them as I picked them.

The light under the natural vault of greenery was restful and dim. As I felt it getting more full of shadows, I started climbing back. I watched as the clouds turned red, and as I reached the garden, it was fun to look at the metamorphosis of the sun, squeezing itself into the oddest shapes before melting into the sea.

The southeast side of the mountain was open to the sun, its slopes used for a few farm houses. Some friends owned a farm, and given some notice, the women in the farmer's family prepared the most spectacular deep-dish pizza. If there had been a recent rain, we'd also get snails. Small and white, they clustered on the thistles that crowded the fields, too rocky to be cultivated.

On the same side there was a cemetery hidden by a forest of prickly pear-cactus and a monastery of *Cappuccini* friars who oversaw the cemetery. Uncle Enzo, a tall, handsome man married to a sister of my mother, had known the friars since he was a young boy and his father had died and had been brought to rest at the monastery.

He went to visit the burial site every now and then, and I didn't mind going along—there was nothing sad about the way the cemetery looked. It was surrounded by ochre walls with a light pink tint. Hand-in-hand with me and my cousin uncle would lead us along the paths while the statues of angels and Madonnas that adorned the crypts tenderly smiled at us. He would pause briefly at the one where his father was buried, his hands tight together and his head down. Then we traced our steps back and outside the gate near the car where we'd find a brown-clad friar with a large basket of prickly pear fruits.

Prickly pears are not the easiest thing to handle: I loved them and I hated them. They are covered with fine spines, which seem to find their way to skin on their own. To minimize the problem when we got home we soaked the fruits in water, washing away most of the prickles. Then we peeled them, using a fork and a sharp knife and with three neat cuts the juicy fruit would be out of its (over)protective skin.

The church used to be very powerful in the village. Sanctuaries dedicated to the cult of pagan deities had been erected in ancient times. As the Normans succeeded in ruling Sicily, churches multiplied; at one time they were said to number six hundred. Very few were open to the public. In some the ceilings had caved in, and the rain and the wind were free to erode the lovely stuccos and the precious marble floors. Wild carnations grew in the cracks of the stones.

Others had been transformed into stores or warehouses; one had been degraded into a movie house, while the adjacent sacristy had been turned into a coffee house. That was the place where I found my very favorite ice cream. The owner of the coffee house was crippled by some disease that had twisted him in a hooklike shape. Still, he busied himself back and forth from the counter to the tables, from the steaming espresso machine to the ice-cream barrel.

A young boy helped him dish out ice cream, and we had surnamed him Gelsomino—Jasmine—as whenever he was asked what flavors he had that was the first he mentioned.

A few years ago when I went back to Erice, I visited Gelsomino. He now owns the bar. The same little glass case is filled with pastries and chocolate bars; two jars on top of it contain prettily wrapped candy and cookies—fennel-seed flavored *mustaccioli*, hard, large, heavy cookies, and customers come in and call him Gelsomino. There have been some changes though: the old man is gone, and the ice-cream barrel has been sacrificed to an electric freezer.

If my brother and I had been particularly good in school, we were rewarded with a trip to somewhere more adventurous than Erice. We'd spend part of the summer in Rome (which was to become my favorite city). We'd wander to northern Italy, stopping in Florence, Pisa, and San Gimignano, where resting became an incredible source of pleasure.

In Rome my admiration was impartially divided between its architectural and historic wonders, and the gastronomic achievements of the restaurants. Eating *pasta e fagioli* and *abbacchio* at La Majella or Artichokes alla Giudeia and *puntarelle* salad at Piperno, I experienced a delight that made me understand for the first time the ancient habit of food offerings to the dead: what else to offer but the one thing, the one pleasure of life that bodyless beings would miss most. When I entered the Pantheon the majestic space in which I found myself took my breath away; I could sense the souls of the Greats were there. If I hadn't been afraid to be mistaken for a loony, I would have repeated the ancient rite, arranging the freshest salad tips, the crunchiest artichokes, and the juiciest slice of a lamb in round clay bowls, placing them on the floor under the very center of the dome of the temple.

After travelling abroad, I was always glad to go back home, and I didn't feel at home until the train arrived in Tuscany where the cultivated hills offered the best welcome. Sometimes I would stop in Florence at my brother's. He was in medical school there, and his house is probably the only place I cooked while I lived in Italy.

Growing up meant also getting married and having to leave. I had to say good-bye to my trips to Rome and to the enjoyment that city offered just by its being there. And I had to say good-bye to the interludes of playing house in Florence. Most painful of all, I had to leave Sicily, my people, a strange mixture of pagan superstitions and wisdom, and my island, full of echoes of nymphs and saints.

An old popular ballad says: "This is the land where birds come, to engage in love games, and sirens come, and sing their songs." Many times as I stood on the shore and watched the sea soothe or sweep the coast punctuated by ancient towers, I felt that if sirens once lived, Sicily would have been the place for them to be.

Instead of their song I heard the music the wind played as it swirled around me, carrying with it goldlike sand from Africa. The *scirocco* played its tune—insinuating itself between the columns of the Greek temples and eroding their tender stone—circled the solitary castles in the inland, and brushed the tops of the palm trees teasing the flowers and the olive tree branches.

I was resigned that in my new home in the United States I stood better chances of finding a perfect imitation of the Coliseum, than a look-alike of a *radicchio* salad.

Without the chatting and the commotion of people around me, I started cooking for my small family. Through food I had the means to recreate smells, colors, and flavors I had left behind; cooking became a way of keeping my identity and made me feel safe as only familiar things can.

I followed the hand written notes I had taken with me, but most of the time I followed my own recollections, repeating gestures seen, reproducing food combinations.

I exchanged letters with my mother. Hers often included a recipe. Homesickness was my best friend and my worst enemy. It helped me keep the old ways, but at the same time it kept me from adapting to the new reality around me. In time I had to admit to myself that a trip to a well-stocked supermarket, in spite of its aseptic appearance, could give much the same results as a trip to the open markets of Palermo. Maybe some vegetables lacked in taste, but a little care and some tricks in preparation would make up for the weaker flavor.

For Sicily and Italy I keep the instinctive attachment of a child to its mother. For my new home I developed the conscious attachment of an adult who can make an evaluation and choice. I no longer seek treasures that are reflections from the past; I create treasures out of what I find.

Introduction

Italians regard food as a source of nutrition, enjoyment, and relaxation—in an interchangeable order of importance.

A very important factor in cooking is being relaxed, and Italian cooking lends itself to this approach. Easy doesn't always mean quick, and difficult is not necessarily time consuming. A simple dish, like *trenette col pesto genovese*, (pasta with basil sauce, from Genoa) can be as good, or better, than a complicated dish and will help build up your experience. No matter how accurate a recipe is and how good the directions are, there is no substitute for the feeling for food you acquire by handling it. If you haven't whipped egg whites or cream, or sautéed onions, you will know the point your egg white was "stiff but not dry," your cream "very stiff," and your onions "aromatic and translucent," only when you have got to the step afterward. Your egg white will be clumped in strange curdles; your cream will be close to butter, and your onions brown—on the way to burned.

In urban areas we are isolated from the reality of food. We're used to seeing food neatly lined up on shelves, in boxes and plastic wraps. It is hard to picture, behind well scrubbed and polished vegetables and fruit, the fields and the orchards where they were grown.

Shopping is a very sanitized event, controlled and without surprises, and can be boring. To enjoy it make the effort to notice colors and shapes, appreciate the bright colors and the freshness of fruits and vegetables. Be receptive to the tenderness of a pink pork loin; let the pungent smell of cheese tickle your palate; and search for any fish that reminds you of the sea.

The ingredients for Italian dishes certainly are not exotic. As a matter of fact, some of the ingredients used most often, like tomatoes, come from the Americas. Any well stocked supermarket in your neighborhood will have what you need to put together a beautiful dinner. Or you can shop for certain items in specialty stores. This type of store doesn't have to label itself Italian; health food stores or Greek, Spanish, or Middle Eastern stores each offer a variety of ingredients used in Italian cooking.

Health food stores are generally well stocked with a variety of nuts, beans, and flour. Greek, Spanish, and Middle Eastern stores have many of the following ingredients: pine nuts, unsalted raw pistachios, black and green olives, saffron, and olive oil. (Other ingredients worth investigating are sugar-coated almonds, plump dried fruit, marzipan, fava beans, chick peas, couscous.)

Greek stores have some shapes of pasta you won't find anywhere else, and the cheese closest to *tuma, queso blanco,* is sold in Latin American stores. As you are shopping, think Italian in terms of quantity and quality, rather than on labels. If you can't afford to buy imported parmesan, or can't find it, buy the American brand. Then to cut down its sweetness, mix in some American romano. Be generous with your food, have plenty on the table, in the pantry, and in the refrigerator. If you want to be economical, you can by taking advantage of plentiful and fresh seasonal foods.

Now you have done all your shopping, but once at home you find out that you are missing an ingredient, or you don't have quite as much as you need. Don't despair—most of the time you can get away with using less of an ingredient, such as onions or parsley, or replacing onions with garlic and parsley with some other herb. Walnuts or almonds may take the place of pine nuts, raisins the place of currants. As you go along in this kind of cooking, you'll choose your ingredients more to your personal liking: the spirit of a dish is sometimes based on the harmony of the ingredients converging together in a pleasant blend; sometimes it is based on the contrast the ingredients generate as they are mixed. As long as you don't disturb that balance or that contrast, you can add your personal touch.

The typical Italian meal consists of a first course (pasta, rice, soups, or a variety of baked dishes); a second course (meat, fish, or eggs, served with a vegetable or two); and dessert (generally fruit, and, occasionally, a sweet pastry).

In a more formal meal *antipasti* might be served before the first course. There will be two "second" courses, more vegetables, and cheese served along with fruit and pastries to end the meal. Bread is always on the table, and, less frequently, bread sticks. Bowls filled with grated cheese are passed around to top pasta and rice. A Sicilian first course sometimes requires toppings other than cheese, like toasted bread crumbs or toasted crushed almonds. Cold water and wine or beer accompany each meal.

Besides salt and pepper shakers, an oil and vinegar cruet will be handy, as often each person dresses his own salad.

An everyday table setting will include a wide rimmed bowl placed on top of a dinner plate; a water glass; a wine glass; a meat or fish knife to the right of the plate; next to the knife a spoon, if one is needed for the first course; two large forks to the left of the plate, and a fruit fork and knife above them. Fruit plates are passed around after the second course. For Italians it is inconceivable to have their first course, especially if pasta, on a plate together with the second course.

Food has to be attractive to the eye, besides having a pleasant smell and taste. Texture becomes an important component, ranging from creamy and fine to firm, from moist to crisp without being runny, chewy, or soggy. What could be more delightful than the crunchy impact of a well-fried light batter followed by the fresh crispness of a vegetable inside? Some raw parsley, finely cut, added to food just before serving, or crushed nuts can bring the dish to life. Pasta, properly cooked, offers to the teeth the right amount of resistance so that chewing takes long enough for the palate to fully enjoy the taste of the sauce that comes with it. Espresso is the best way to complete an Italian meal. Served in small quantities, its strong flavor works over the tastes left behind by the different courses and keeps them from lingering in the mouth. It won't work miracles if you have eaten too much, but at least psychologically one feels purified.

Notes on Herbs, Spices, and Basic Ingredients

Herbs are best when fresh. In Sicily herbs have a place in gardens along with the flowers and trees. Entire garden edges are made of rosemary, and oregano bushes grow near lemon verbenas, geraniums, and cactuses. Potted basil decorates window sills, courtyards, and balconies: its small leaves grow tightly together to form perfectly round domes. Herbs seem to grow effortlessly. Caper plants spring out among rocks and cliffs along the coast: their edible part—the buds—bloom into delicate flowers. Wild fennel prefers a cooler climate and dots the mountain sides with its umbrellalike flowers. Bay-leaf trees flank walkways, casting a scentful shade.

Treat your ingredients gently; don't chop them away—slamming a huge knife up and down on the butcher block. They are not enemies to be disintegrated; they are fragile things to be reduced to smaller sizes, and you can do that with very little energy and a sharp medium-to-small knife. Cut and slice, so you won't break up the fibers and disperse the juices.

Properly dried, most herbs retain much of their essence and can be used in place of fresh ones when these aren't available.

Oregano is one herb that I find has an unpleasant bite when just picked from the plant, and I only use it dry.

Dry herbs and spices have a good shelf life, but with time they lose their bite and their essence. Buy them in small quantities and keep them dry and cool.

Saffron, if in the form of whole stigmas, has to be crushed and softened in small amounts of broth or water before use.

Capers are best when preserved in salt but are hard to find this way. Capers in vinegar are available in any market. Whether preserved in salt or in vinegar, wash and soak them in water before you use them, unless the recipe gives other instructions.

Celery ought to be free from brown spots on the outside, and looking at the leaves in the core, they shouldn't show any sign of deterioration. Use the outer ribs for soups, and the heart, including its leaves, for dishes like *caponata*. While celery ribs aren't bursting with flavor, they are good for texture. The leaves contribute the distinctive celery taste.

You can use either yellow or white onions. Select the ones that feel the most firm and don't show traces of mold on the outside. Red onions are my favorites, but they are harder to find. If in cutting an onion you uncover some mushy layers, make sure you cut that part off—it can ruin your dish with its rotten taste and smell. Discard the sprout if there is one.

Garlic can surprise you. There is no sure way of knowing if your garlic, instead of having white plump cloves, will have shrivelled-up yellowish ones. Choose large heads that feel "full." When peeling the cloves, cut off any part that has turned brown.

Other flavorings used in the recipes are nuts, olives, dried mushrooms (fresh mushrooms are too watery and should only be used as vegetables), tomato paste, anchovies, currants, jasmine flowers, lemon peel, orange peel (both fresh and candied), candied citron, candied papaya (to replace candied squash), and semisweet chocolate. Recipes may call for orange and lemon juice, in addition to oil, red wine vinegar, wine, liqueur, vodka, brandy, and vanilla extract. Black pepper is used abundantly to spice up dishes; at times it is replaced by small, hot red peppers, whole or crushed. Spices and herbs, like nutmeg, cloves, saffron, mint, and marjoram, are used very sparingly. Others, like parsley, seem to find their way, in large quantity, to many dishes. Salt is added to allow flavor to reach its highest point.

The salt called for throughout this book is common table salt. Food in Italy is well seasoned with salt, either added in the kitchen while cooking or sprinkled on afterward and given the time to sink in. Salt at the table is used sparingly.

In the United States I have found that food gets to the table undersalted. Individually adding salt works for some dishes. It can be very satisfactory to chew and work the salt into a bite of steak, while in some cases, like pasta or mayonnaise, salt needs to sink in. Sprinkling it from a shaker will keep the taste of salt right on the surface: it will be the first to greet you and will overpower the other tastes of the dish.

When buying nuts in bulk, check that they are not stale or rancid. If you see grainy webs clinging to them, turn to another store or to canned nuts. Almonds are pretty resilient to deterioration; walnuts, on the other hand, turn rancid very easily. Pistachios are the most delicate to keep; this is why you seldom find them raw, and they are commonly sold roasted and salted.

Green olives, whether out of a can or a barrel in a specialty store, carry a strong brine taste. Soak them in water, changing it a few times.

Dried mushrooms have to be inspected carefully for sand and mud. After keeping them in water for one hour, they'll have plumped up enough to tell where the stems are. Rub off any sand or mud you find on the stems while the mushrooms are immersed in water. Then, take the mushrooms out of the water, change the water, and return the mushrooms to it. Repeat the procedure more than once if you find any debris. (If you drain them by pouring water and mushrooms into a colander, the dirt will be poured back onto the mushrooms, so it is best to remove the mushrooms by hand.) Two hours of soaking should be enough to ready the mushrooms for use. In the last hour don't change the water, and reserve it after you have removed the mushrooms for the last time. The water will have a strong flavor, and you might find a use for it in your dish. The mushrooms will be about triple in size and have a rubbery consistency.

Tomato paste comes in tubes (very handy if you use small amounts at a time and wish to refrigerate the rest) and cans. You can transfer the unused portion to a glass jar, pack it down well, and as an added precaution pour enough olive oil over it to cover the surface. It will keep for a couple of weeks.

Use anchovies in their plainest form, flat fillets with no additions but oil, preferably olive. Discard the oil.

Lemons and oranges get to vendors and markets stamped, and lemons, in addition to the stamp, carry a smell other than their natural one. The average shopper who may have never smelled a fresh lemon probably thinks that the scent of a lemon is not worth whiffing twice. I like to think that giving lemons a good scrub will eliminate some of the chemical, probably a preservative, and some of its smell. Softness in lemons and oranges doesn't indicate that they are ripe, but, rather, that they are not fresh.

Olive oil is crucial to *all* Italian cooking. Olive trees grow in southern Mediterranean countries. In Sicily you can see them on the countryside, some centuries old. They stand isolated or in orchards neatly marked by dry stone walls, in gardens, or against columns of Greek temples.

Their trunks are slit, marred with cavities. From their troubled mass new branches shoot out, incredibly supple, ready to bend without breaking under the weight of their fruit. Their leaves are oval, small, and slender. They offer a dark leathery surface to the sun, but underneath they seem dusted with dull silver. The choicest fruit is picked for eating; the fruit to keep green is put in brine; others are kept in containers with good drainage and frequently tossed around, and in time they will become black olives.

Smaller olives are used for their oil. There are different systems used, and the best oil is obtained by the first extraction with a cold press. Successive extractions will give a lower quality and higher acid product.

The first oil extracted—fresh, pure, and unrefined—bears the concentrated taste, color, and smell of the olives. Eating it, soaked into dark bread, trickled on vegetables, or mixed with pasta, garlic, and cheese, is a unique experience.

Olive oil is the only kind an Italian cook will consider for use with a vegetable, any dish where it will be blended in with other ingredients, or for pasta sauce.

Oil from seeds, corn, sunflower, and other sources, is used largely for deep frying food coated with flour, breadcrumbs, or a batter, or for deep frying uncoated food with low absorbency. As long as the oil from seeds stays on the surface, forming a crust, it is considered acceptable. Oil from seeds, highly refined and practically tasteless and odorless, is found acceptable by some as a condiment. Sometimes they may complement olive oil, as in making mayonnaise. Used along with olive oil, it will turn out a sauce lighter in texture and taste than if using only olive oil.

Choose a brand of olive oil with a low grade of acidity. If in a can, it is always best to transfer the oil to a glass container, especially if you are not going to consume it in a few weeks. Keep it away from heat sources.

The other indispensable ingredient to Italian cooking is canned peeled tomatoes. There are plenty of cans to choose from. Shelves in the markets show a variety of labels with Italian names, promising Italian shaped tomatoes, tomatoes with Italian ancestry, or patriotic tomatoes with white, red, and green backgrounds claiming to be Italian style.

When you open the can and get the tomatoes out, you are

confronted by one, or all, of the following: very few tomatoes and lots of juice, tomatoes that disintegrate into a pulp and make the task of removing the seeds almost impossible, tomatoes so acidic that it will take extra salt and even some sugar to make them palatable, or tomatoes in good number, good shape, fleshy and firm.

Patiently test different brands, starting with the cheapest—as long as the label has two words on it: *peeled* and *tomatoes*. It helps to shake a few cans gently next to your ear. To select one wait for a full plop rather than a squash. If you use only part of the tomatoes after opening the can, refrigerate the rest in a glass container covered in the juice they were packed in, and plan to use them within a few days.

Currants, on every market shelf from autumn through Christmas, become a scarce item after that season. Keep an extra box, well-sealed, in the refrigerator. Currants dry out easily and at some point, no matter how carefully you keep them, become very grainy in consistency. Don't let this prevent you from using them, though, since cooking makes it unnoticeable.

Jasmine flowers are hard to find. If you happen to live in a warm and temperate climate, you might come across a jasmine vine. The flowers are small and white with starlike petals. Their scent is delicate, between a rose and a magnolia. Pick the blossoms that are just starting to open at night or very early morning and insert a few in a watermelon pudding, about three or four per serving.

Citron, candied, appears with the Christmas related goods and disappears with them. It keeps for a while in the refrigerator. Health food stores generally have good supplies of papayas that I call candied and they call honey-dipped.

Semisweet chocolate bits can be made from any plain candy bar or you can buy the baking kind. Chocolate drops may do the job, if you don't want to reduce the chocolate to bits by cutting it. They are just a bit too big and offer no surprises so far as size.

Wheat flour is one of the foundations on which Italian cook-ing is built. Some Italians will swear that in no day in their lives have they missed eating a plate of pasta nor has their table been without bread.

Only Sicilians, one day a year, may abstain from eating any refined wheat product. The reason for it is explained in a story I was told as a child.

Quite a few centuries ago there was a famine. People of Siracusa had gathered together in their cathedral, a very un-usual church ingeniously built within the structure of a Greek temple. They were addressing their prayers to the patroness of the city, Santa Lucia, and as they were praying someone noticed that a dove, which had flown in through one of the high, narrow windows, bore in her beak a wheat ear.

People flocked out of the cathedral and discovered on the shore a ship wreck; a recent storm had beached a cargo boat filled with wheat. People were hungry and couldn't wait for the mill to make flour, so the first meal they ate was the whole plain kernels. To this day on the date celebrating the saint, in most houses whole wheat kernels are cooked, and quite a few people do not eat anything made from flour.

Wheat is tied to many images of mine from the past. Going out of town, it didn't take long before I could see fields of wheat covering the ground for miles, changing from the tender green of the early sprouts in the spring to the yellow gold of the ripe ears in the summer. We went to the country near harvest time. I walked along the edge of this dry sea, brushing against it, enjoying its ticklish contact.

To look over the wheat and see it bend with the breeze was one of my happiest sights. It stemmed concern that a rain might come before the harvesting machine, and the clear sky was searched for any sign of it. The adults were relieved when the crop was harvested and put in storage, while I couldn't bear the sight of the yellow stiff stumps left on the bare ground.

As the soil was turned over, it took a more reassuring look.

After the first rain spots of wild flowers would peak through the big clumps of chocolate brown earth, and it looked like an ideal bed for the newly sown wheat to rest on through the winter.

Here we have plenty of flour to use for pasta, breads, and pastries. Of all flours unbleached is the one that works best in my recipes, as it can be used for thickening a sauce, or making pasta, or baking. Semolina flour is the best kind to use to coat fried foods.

Notes on Pasta

De Pasta, or About Pasta

Pasta is basically a very simple dish that rises to many degrees of sophistication through various manipulations of the dough and by the addition of different sauces.

People in Italy are generations away from the time when they spent hours every day preparing food. It was hard work for the mammas, and commercial pasta started being used for daily consumption as soon as industrial mills started producing it affordably, decades ago. The habit of making pasta at home remained on farms and villages, where life is much slower than in cities. Nowadays pasta making is a happening; it is done for fun rather than as a chore, and it is a special treat to everybody.

Homemade Pasta

The plainest homemade pasta dough combines water with almost any kind of wheat flour—bleached, unbleached, whole —also used are fine tender wheat flour, and coarser durum wheat flour (semolina).

A more elaborate pasta will combine refined wheat flour with eggs and water. Sometimes spinach is added in place of water to make green pasta.

Many other elaborations of pasta—with tomatoes, artichokes, and unusual ingredients—have been used in very recent times. These new concoctions might be interesting, but they are rather unorthodox and a distortion of what pasta is meant to be: a subdued medium that easily agrees with any flavor it carries.

There are electric machines available for home use that will knead, roll, and shape the pasta with little more effort than just measuring the ingredients. With all the labor gone some of the fun goes too; one may as well buy pasta in one of the many stores that make it daily. However, fresh pasta made with electric machines, at home or from a store, tends to be too soft and doesn't hold up too well during cooking.

One of the essentials for good pasta al dente is to begin with very stiff dough. Kneading it by hand is hard, but it does have positive side effects: it is good exercise and you won't have to count the calories in your pasta helping.

Rolling out a stiff dough is made easier by using a machine. Turn a handle around and around and nice, smooth pasta sheets come out. Change the setting on the handle, turn some more, and your pasta comes out neatly cut.

Commercial Pasta

Any, or almost any, commercial pasta available on a supermarket shelf can be acceptable if cooked properly.

I use Mueller, San Giorgio, and Safeway brand along with Buitoni, *Barilla*, and *De Cecco* and get very good results from all of them. One almost sure way of ending up with a slimy or a lumpy pasta is to follow *ad litteram* the instructions on cooking time given by any recipe, while forgetting to stir.

Pasta made exclusively from durum wheat (semolina) will take the longest time to cook and will have a more chewy texture. As the quantity of semolina decreases so does the cooking time. The shape of pasta is also a factor in determining a longer or shorter cooking period.

The best way to determine if the pasta is done, or close to being done, is to trust your ability in detecting texture through touching, watching, and tasting.

While time is an element that is nearly impossible to establish in cooking pasta, there are some simple procedures and expedients that will help to obtain a good *pasta al dente*.

One pound of pasta will do very well in 11 to 12 cups of water. If you are cooking long pasta, like spaghetti, linguine, tagliatelle, etc., break it in half; it will make your life much easier while you are cooking it and when you are going to eat it. Add 1½ tablespoons salt to the water and bring it to a rolling boil over high heat; I advise to use a long fork to stir if the pasta is long, as the teeth of the fork will help loosen it up.

Add pasta to the boiling water and start stirring immediately. After one or two minutes of stirring well down to the bottom center, sides, and from the bottom up, cover the pot. As it reaches a boil again, remove the lid, stir, and keep the heat high enough for the water to boil without overflowing. Stir occasionally. After a few minutes start checking on the consistency. Pasta shouldn't be hanging limp from your fork; cut some and check the section. As long as you see a distinct white core, pasta is not done. When the white core has almost disappeared and the texture is satisfactory to your taste, but still a bit on the hard side, your pasta is ready to be drained. Add some cold water to the pot; this will prevent further softening due to the steam while in the colander. Drain. Reserve some water and mix it at once with your sauce. Use a wide, shallow serving dish, rather than one deep and narrow as this will prevent pasta from lumping together and losing texture. To loosen up pasta you might add some reserved water.

Eat your pasta right away; very few pastas can afford sitting on a plate even for a short time without losing some of their qualities.

Before you decide what shape of pasta to use or if it's to be commercial or fresh, give some thought to the sauce you'll serve with it. Plain commercial pasta will go with any sauce, while fresh pasta will be especially enhanced by cream sauces, tomato sauces, and meat sauces.

One peculiarity of the Italian taste—only the plainest commercial pasta is acceptable with fish sauces—(no egg, no spinach, no whole wheat, no fresh pasta, etc.).

To get the idea of the importance of pasta shapes, think of trying to eat spaghetti with a simple sauce of peas and oil.Can you see all those little green balls slither down to the bottom of the plate? Instead, now picture eating *ditalini* or shells with the same sauce: see all the little rascals trapped in the pasta openings, with nowhere to run but into your mouth?

As for the amount of pasta to cook, consider how rich and/or bulky your sauce is going to be. Three-quarters of a pound of pasta with a plain sauce is a good quantity to share among four; for people who eat small quantities you might stretch it to serve six. If, among your guests or your family, there is a pasta glutton, cook more pasta or pass the serving dish to the big eater last!

To conclude, here is a pasta story overheard in Palermo.

Two women on a bus were talking to each other about their families and their children. One seemed very distressed and was complaining how difficult it was to please her children and how they aggravated her.

The other woman listened with real sympathy and then told her anecdote. Everyday she asked her children—and she had lots of children—what kind of pasta they wished to have for dinner. Invariably they all picked different kinds. One wanted ziti, one rigatoni, one penne, one spaghetti. Not even once did a couple of them agree on the same shape.

One day, having asked the same question and got the same dissenting answers, she marked down all the different pastas.

When it was time to have dinner, she threw in the big pot of boiling water a handful of this, a handful of that, and a handful of the other, and so on, satisfying the request of each child.

Then she brought the pasta to the table. "Mamma, what did you do?" was the horrified cry of the children. "I did exactly what you asked for: Peppino, you asked for shells, there they are. Ninuzzo, you asked for ziti, they are there too. Everything you asked for is there. Now, *scartativilli.*" Or, "pick it out yourselves."

Notes on Dairy Products, Vegetables, and Meats

Dairy Products

In urban areas dairy products' freshness are out of our control. The only measure of age we can have is a date stamped somewhere on the container.

Searching for that can be a little disturbing. Every time I turn over a carton of eggs, I'm anxious that it might come open and unload all twelve eggs at my feet. When I look at dates on cream containers, I get distressed realizing that cream bought at Thanksgiving can be used at Christmas.

Discounting my uneasiness about cream longevity, American chickens and cows do a great job of laying eggs and producing milk. On the whole, dairy products on supermarket shelves are very good and void of surprises.

Cream

Heavy cream bought in stores is a little too thin, but don't blame the cows—blame the people who process it and take out a little too much of the fat content. Whip it shortly before you need it, using a very cold bowl and a chilled electric beater. Don't stop whipping when it is airy and fluffy; keep beating it until it starts losing some volume and looks like it might turn into butter. That is when you stop.

Ricotta

Fresh ricotta is always watery and traditionally was placed in tightly woven baskets to give the whey a chance to run.

Packed in tight containers, the liquid has nowhere to run, so it is a good practice to let the ricotta sit in a strainer lined with cheesecloth preferably overnight to get rid of the unwanted moisture.

Often American ricotta has a grainy texture. Used in dishes other than desserts the texture doesn't matter, but for desserts it should be beaten a long time to make it as smooth as possible.

Butter

Butter is an ingredient used in many Italian dishes. It is never salted and has no artificial coloring. I disagree with the assessment often heard about Italian cuisine that northern style is lighter, relying heavily on the use of butter and cream, and that southern style is heavier, giving preference to the use of tomatoes and olive oil. Cream and butter may be lighter in color than oil and tomatoes, but certainly they are not lighter on the system.

The differentiation of cuisine among Italian regions was established long ago. Dishes were based on what the land offered and influenced by different cultural backgrounds. In the south, and especially in Sicily, we are blessed with sun and warm weather. Olive trees thrive and are plentiful, while pastures for cattle are not. In the past olive oil was the main fat used in cooking, and butter was a luxury, used sparingly. In the north the facts were reversed. The climate allowed the raising of cattle, and butter, readily available, was the main fat used.

Today, with the easing of communications, the development of different agricultural criteria, and the growing awareness of the reflection of diet on health, the cuisine is getting pretty much leveled off with the exception of some very traditional dishes that have maintained their individuality and that can be unmistakably placed.

Basic dairy products, such as eggs, milk, cream, ricotta, and some well-known and aged Italian cheeses, like *parmigiano* and *pecorino*, are readily available and acceptable. However, there are a number of Italian cheeses that are either unknown or known in forms very far from what they are in their country of origin.

Take mozzarella, a very commonly used ingredient in Italian dishes, and, as found in local markets, a sad case. Mozzarella should ooze milk, be pure white, melt in your mouth, and at the same time be a consistency that produces a little squeak when chewed. Instead what you get is a yellowing lump, which could be hit with a baseball bat and still make it through a whole game unscarred.

If you want to make one of those wonderful salads of slices of tomatoes and mozzarella mixed with basil leaves and olive oil, you have to search your neighborhood and hope to find a little mamma and papa store that makes it daily in the back room.

Other cheeses, such as *stracchino, robbiola,* and *mascarpone,* are highly perishable. Still, some stores do carry them; try the food section of large department stores as well as asking for them in local cheese shops.

Cheese to be grated should be kept well wrapped in wax paper and aluminum foil, and the wrapping should be changed often. In addition to the covering, a thin layer of olive oil spread on parmesan, romano, or caciocavallo, will help to keep the cheese from drying out and molding. Once grated, cheese should be used up, as it won't maintain its qualities as well as the whole chunk.

Various Cheeses

Less perishable cheese, like Bel Paese, Gorgonzola, and Fontina, can be found in local markets, but it is generally past its peak. Bel Paese and Fontina are often dry, and Gorgonzola overly ripe.

If you find a market that has a good variety of Italian cheeses, ask to have them cut from the wheel. If the first slice looks dry—or soggy—don't buy it. Ask to taste a small piece after the first slice is removed. Good cheese should have no bitter aftertaste and should be pleasant, no matter how strong.

Gorgonzola should be creamy, and with its Brie and blue cheese taste it shouldn't be overpowering.

Italian cheeses have suffered from poor imitations and bad press. A cheese to be good doesn't have to be French. (I can't resist adding at this point, that the same statement applies to wine and cooking.)

Vegetables

Shopping for vegetables is much simpler than shopping for cheeses, since produce counters overflow in all seasons. Most of the time the vegetables have no blemishes and burst with health. Take a little care in picking them out, and you will come very close to the quality that you would get from homegrown vegetables. Vegetables such as eggplants, zucchini, and cucumbers are more likely to have too many seeds when they are large; choose the skinniest ones with bright colors and unwrinkled skins that are firm to the touch. The very small "Italian" eggplant, about three inches long, is seldom used in Italy; eggplant used in everyday cooking is larger, about five inches long, and not quite as bitter as the others.

Leafy vegetables should look fresh, with no wilted leaves. Celery, cauliflower, and cultivated mushrooms should show no discoloration. Pick mushrooms where membrane caps are close around the stem.

Peppers should be fleshy. Try to evaluate their weight in relation to their size. Wild and garden asparagus, the green variety, are used very widely in Italy, in first and second courses and in side dishes. In the garden variety of asparagus the size doesn't have much to do with tenderness. Look at their color, from the tip to the end, choosing the ones with the most green. To insure even cooking, pick similar sizes. Reject spindly spears and ones that show ridges down the stem, no matter the color.

Meats

Years ago, while I was in Italy, I met some Americans who lived there. They did their shopping through Sears and Roebuck catalogues and for their food supplies relied on periodical trips to a Navy base, a few hours away from town.

They got packages of orderly lined-up steaks, frozen, of course. So perfectly equal were they that they seemed to be stamped out with a mold. The steaks were speckled with white and surrounded by fat.

That, together with their habits of eating bacon, eggs fried in bacon fat, pancakes with scoops of butter and drowned in syrup, bread and butter, not to mention lemon meringue and pecan pies, made me wonder about their judgment; they accused pasta of being the culprit of their extra pounds and chins.

Italians do not rely on animal fat to produce tender meat. Instead, they place great importance on the proper feeding of young animals and techniques in cutting, preparing, and cooking the meat to insure its tenderness.

A meat counter generally doesn't carry prepackaged meat cut the way you need it, but it will have plenty of pieces of roasts, round, rump, eye of the round, veal legs, etc. With the cooperation of the butcher, you can choose your own piece of meat and have it cut as you wish. Eye of the round, when pink, and sliced thin, can be as tender as the veal that is most commonly used in Italy. Thick steaks are very uncommon in Italy. There are a few exceptions, for example the *costate alla fiorentina*, that is, rib steaks as they are cut in Florence and served grilled.

What is sold here as lamb in Italy would be considered young mutton. It is very tasty and tender but gamier than a small lamb, whose flesh is more delicate than milk-fed veal.

Chickens, as they are raised today, are usually the same, whatever their nationality. They are a typical example of a dilemma of modern life, having to choose larger quantity and affordable prices over finer quality and higher prices.

Pork in Italy is eaten primarily during the winter months. Italians seem to experiment with pork more than with any meat. Turning it into sausage is the simplest method of preparation. Pork is preserved in an innumerable variety of ways. Every part of the pig is used, economically and efficiently, from the ears to the tail. Salami, prosciutti, capocolli, and *cotechini* are turned out. Maybe because of such dedication to preserving, fresh pork in Italy is available only in a limited number of cuts, compared to what the market offers here. Use rosy chops and roasts, fresh and juicy to make *ragù*; cut thin slices of loin for cutlets and scaloppine or roast it in the oven or cook it in a pot; with leftover roast make sandwiches or a stew. Pork is a nice alternative to other meats and can be fixed to be part of a sophisticated meal. Served without the addition of barbecue sauces, apples, or prunes, its taste will be very new to most palates.

Notes on Fish and Seafood

Fish and seafood are items that do not appear on the American table as often as they should and with good reason. Truly fresh fish and seafood are hard to get and easy to ruin with improper cooking. A bite of fresh fish (that has been out of its natural element for no longer than twenty-four hours) should bring you the same kind of sensation as being on a shore, breathing salty air. The taste should be clean and delicate, with an iodine undertone, like the smell of fresh seaweed.

In the area where I live, salmon, flounder, rockfish, and some other finned fish are relatively easy to find fresh. Squid, shrimp, and tuna are not.

Some fish, frozen—and defrosted—in the proper fashion, although losing the characteristics that make fresh fish so desirable, will not acquire the smell and corresponding taste of unclean (not yet gutted) fish left in the sun. Squid and shrimp, when fresh, smell like the ocean, but they develop a fishy odor once frozen and then defrosted. A particularly pungent fish odor in frozen finned and shellfish often indicates improper defrosting and/or refrigeration.

Even good markets sell frozen fish but don't expect the seller to volunteer any information about the unnatural state his merchandise went through. Unless specifically asked, he'll keep it to himself.

Therefore, ask very direct questions. Was the fish frozen? How long was the fish refrigerated? Do they have a fish a little younger in the back?

If you want fillets, avoid the ones on display. Pick your own with head, tail and fins still attached and have it prepared as you wish. If you want steak fish, ask to have it freshly cut, unless the one in the display case has an unmistakable just-sliced look. Don't take the first slice, as it is often frost bitten and dried out.

The way the fish looks can tell you a lot about how fresh it is. In finned fish look for iridescence all over, firmly attached scales, "clean" eyes—looking ready to pop out, and red gills.

In squid look for unbroken skin, shimmering with definite reddish-brown specks. The hoods shouldn't be limp.

Shrimp shells should be solid: no part should be flaking off. Pick them from the tail and see if they are firm.

When you cook fish, handle it gently. Use a spatula to turn it, so that it won't break apart. Don't overcook it; to test for doneness don't poke it and stick it with forks that would only let the juices run out, and not tell you much. In the case of small fish or steak fish, more often than not you run the risk of overcooking, as they cook very fast. With fish (large and small) baked whole, respect the cooking times given in the recipes, and five minutes before the end of the cooking period insert a spatula corner along the side of the fish, where the dorsal fins run, just in between the fillets; if the flesh detaches itself easily from the bone, the fish is done. With steak fish, respect cooking times and trust your eye. You can flake it with a fork. If it flakes easily, it is done.

If you have cooked a whole fish, do not feel that you have to fillet it before serving it. A whole fish is very impressive, and easy to make portions out of it. To serve, run a fish knife or a dull edged spatula along the sides where the fillets meet, pulling out the line of small bones that divides them.

Then, part the top fillet lengthwise along the middle. Ease the spatula crosswise, so that the fillet is divided in four parts or more. (I am assuming you are dealing with a good-size fish.) As you have served the top fillet, break the central bone at the head and tail, lift it, and divide the bottom fillet the same way. Let your family and your guests entertain themselves removing the small bones and the skin.

We all have our preferences to what part of fowl or beef we like best. Eating fish is no different. The tail is always the driest and lightest in flavor. The area around the stomach has the strongest flavor. The plumpest and most tender part is right below the head. And right in the head there are the best morsels, the cheeks. They are to fish what filet mignon is to beef.

Fish recipes have been the hardest to adapt to what the market offers in the United States. The ocean doesn't seem to give fish the same taste as the Mediterranean waters.

Markets will clean most fish, but some they will not, and you will have to. Here are simple notes on squid and mussels cleaning.

Cleaning and Preparing Squid

Get hold of the tentacles right where they meet with the hood and pull them. Some of the digestive tract will come off along with the ink bladder (sac). Easy to identify, the digestive tract and ink bladder are softer and different in color from the hood and the tentacles. Remove and discard them, keeping the ink sac if the recipe calls for it. Handle the sac carefully; it is very fragile. Remove the beaklike cartilage located where the tentacles join. The cartilage is easy to uncover turning the tentacles up and spreading them.

Clean any jellylike substance out from the hood. On the front of the hood, running along the middle, there is a thin transparent cartilage. Remove it by gently pulling the tip you can feel by running your fingers around the inside of the hood opening, right at its edge. Make sure you remove any of the digestive tract that might still be attached to the tentacles.

Run a good deal of water in the hood and rinse the tentacles well. If the squid doesn't have a fishy smell after you blot out the water, it is ready to be used. If the squid still has a strong smell, bring some water to a boil, dip the squid in it for a few seconds until it starts turning white, drain it and rinse it in cold water. Blot out as much water as you can, and use as directed in the recipe.

There is no need to remove the skin, as it isn't tough and doesn't have an unpleasant texture.

Cleaning and Preparing Mussels

When buying mussels, as any other shellfish or fish, go to a reliable store. It might be more expensive but will pay off. Sometime mussels ingest sand and retain it: consequently, they become pearl logged. The pearls are not precious enough to sell, but they are hard enough to break a tooth. Make sure that your mussels don't contain any. Request that a mollusk be opened for you at the fish store. (Not all stores will comply.) Feel the mollusk with your finger and look at it carefully. The surface will be rough if there are pearls.

Soak the mussels in a mixture of water, salt, and cornmeal (1 gallon water, 1 cup cornmeal, and ⅓ cup salt) for 1 hour.

Scrub them with a hard brush and pull out the seaweed visible between the shell halves. Discard any mussels that are open and won't close when touched. They are definitely dead and possibly full of mud. Place the mussels in a very large skillet in no more than two layers. Cover it, place it on medium high heat, and shake the pan frequently. After five minutes check the mussels. Remove any that have opened and look somewhat firm. Keep the pan on the heat and keep shaking it, checking and removing the open mussels every minute.

Some can be very stubborn and will need quite a bit of heat before opening up. The ones that do not open after twenty minutes are most likely dead and must be discarded.

Mussels are ready when moist, plump, and barely detached from the shell. Leaving them on the heat too long after they open up dries them out and shrinks them. If you want to remove them from the shells, you might find it convenient to use a half shell as a scoop to detach them. Pull out any remains of the weed cord left in the mollusk, that was their attachment to the cluster.

According how you plan to use them, you might want to keep the juice collected in the pan, and you might want to reserve some shells.

Strain the juice through a sieve lined with a cheesecloth. Scrub the shells. Keep both the juice and the shells refrigerated until ready for use.

General Recipe Structure and Content

The number of people served and the serving size indicated in the recipes is based on the assumption that a three-course dinner is being prepared (and that you have an Italian appetite). The amount of sauce allowed is strictly in the Italian taste and tradition.

The ingredients list in each recipe is arranged according to preparation requirements.

Remember that:

- vegetables are always sorted, cleaned, and peeled, unless otherwise stated;
- chickens used are large fryers;
- flour is measured unsifted;
- sugar mentioned in the recipes is white and granulated, unless otherwise stated;
- breadcrumbs are plain, with no flavorings;
- wines used are never cooking wines but are table wines;
- water is tap at room temperature, unless otherwise stated.

In the recipe directions:

- the cooking time can vary quite a bit, given quality and quantity of the food, different cooking vessels, burner size, fuel quality, frequency of stirring;
- most of the dishes do not swim in liquid; the meats are well browned, sauces and soups are thick;
- sometime to correct the taste of the dish that is not quite right, the only thing needed is to reduce the liquid;
- adjust the cooking time to your means, if necessary;
- use wooden spoons to stir; keep some for desserts only;
- use ungreased bakeware, unless otherwise stated;
- gadgets are welcome if they help to cut down the time involved in preparing the food and improve its quality;
- to cut vegetables I prefer the use of sharp knives to gadgets. Knives need not be fancy and expensive. Inexpensive knives can easily be kept sharp. I sharpen mine with an electric sharpener. After years of such treatment my five-and-ten-cent-store knives are still in good shape.
- food processors are great to: grind solid ingredients for pesto; grate cheese; turn nuts into paste; make pâtés; slice potatoes; make any sauce where ingredients need pureeing, puree any food;
- counter-top mixers like the Kitchen Aid K5-A are a pleasure for kneading soft doughs, mixing, and whipping. The food being prepared doesn't get overheated or overpulverized, and a mixer is much easier to control than a food processor; also blenders make good pesto;
- manual pasta machines such as the Atlas Modello 150 Lusso, provide a relief from rolling out stiff doughs; use them for pasta and for any similar consistency pastry dough.

Note: The recipe names are given in Italian and in English. Words hyphenated within the Italian recipe names are mostly Sicilian dialect words.

Recipes

Hors D'Oeuvres
Antipasti

Antipasti

Antipasti are generally served at room temperature; exceptions will be indicated in the recipes. A must for all antipasti: plenty of bread available at the table. The bread, Italian or French, unless otherwise stated in the recipes, should be served at room temperature, cut in chunks.

A great number of antipasti have a good refrigerator life; they'll keep for a few days without losing in flavor; in fact, they might improve. As a rule, antipasti in a vinegar-based sauce are very resistant to spoilage, as are olives and fish preserved in any of the conventional ways, such as in oil, smoked, or salted.

In deciding what antipasti can be made ahead of time, or in larger quantities and kept in the refrigerator, use your common sense and common knowledge of what foods are more susceptible to spoilage. In most antipasti recipes there is no indication of how many they'll serve, the reason being that antipasti are served in combinations. Keeping that in mind, quantities in each recipe are such that any assortment of four will serve four to six people.

Some of the dishes in the second course recipes and in the side dish recipes are commonly used also as antipasti.

Second course recipes:
Stuffed peppers *(peperoni imbottiti)*
Stuffed onions *(cipolle ripiene)*

Butterflied sardines *(sarde "a linguata")*
Butterflied sardines in sweet and sour sauce *(sarde agrodolce)*
Mackerel in oil *(sgombro sott'olio)*
Sea salad *(insalata di mare)*

Side dish recipes:
Baked zucchini *(zucchine infornate)*
Baked onions halves *(mezze cipolle infornate)*
Caramelized pearl onions *(cipollette caramellate)*
Peppers with breadcrumbs *(peperoni al pan grattato)*
Stuffed artichokes *(carciofi ripieni)*
Artichokes and asparagus cold plate *(piatto freddo di carciofi e asparagi)*
Artichokes, peas, and fava beans, in sweet and sour sauce *(frittella)*
Eggplants parmigiana *(melanzane alla parmigiana)*
Fried Eggplant *(caponata)*
Roasted eggplants *(melanzane arrostite)*

OLIVE NERE CONDITE

Dressed Black Olives

Olives: ½ pound black, Greek or Sicilian
Rosemary: 1 teaspoon, leaves
Oil: olive

Mix the olives with just enough oil to coat them. Mix in the rosemary.
Note:
You may also try the hot version. Warm up some oil in a heavy skillet. Add to it the olives and the rosemary, stir them for a few minutes over medium heat until thoroughly hot. Serve while still hot.

OLIVE VERDI CONDITE

Dressed Green Olives

Olives: ½ pound green, Greek or Sicilian. Crush them slightly
    with a heavy object (the flat side of a meat tenderizer)
Celery: 1 heart, the very center of it, cut in small pieces; use also
    the leafy part and some of the leaves of the outer ribs, as
    they have more flavor
Garlic: 2 cloves, crushed in their jackets
Red pepper: ¼ to ½ teaspoon, dried hot chili, crushed
Oil: olive, ⅓ to ½ cup

Mix all the ingredients in a tight-fitting bowl.

    Let them stand a few hours at room temperature before serving, stirring every now and then. For best results refrigerate and let marinate 24 hours; stir them a few times during this time.

FILETTI DI ACCIUGA CON L'ACETO

Anchovies with Vinegar

Anchovies: 2 ounce can, oil preserved, flat fillets; drain the oil
    well
Vinegar: wine
Oregano: 1 teaspoon
Garlic: 4 cloves, crushed in their jackets

Cover the anchovies with vinegar; add the oregano and the garlic, mix gently, and let them marinate overnight.

PROSCIUTTO E FICHI

Prosciutto and Figs

Prosciutto: ¼ pound, sliced very thin; fat removed
Figs: 1 pound ripe and peeled

Wrap thin ribbons of prosciutto around the figs.
  Serve barely chilled.

PEPERONI SOTT'OLIO

Peppers in Oil

Peppers: 4 bell, green or red or yellow: they must be very fresh
    and very "fleshy"
Oil: olive, ¼ cup
Salt: to taste
Pepper: freshly ground black, to taste

Optional:
Parsley: 4 full sprigs, cut very finely; discard the stems
Garlic: 1 clove, cut in minute pieces

Preheat oven to 400°F. Wash the peppers and place them on a
cookie sheet with very shallow sides.
  Bake 1 hour and 10 minutes or until most of the peppers'
surface shows brown spots and wrinkled spots. Turn them once
during the baking time.
  Remove from the oven and let them get cold. Peel them,

remove the stems, and cut them in half, lengthwise. Remove the seeds. Cut the peppers into wide strips, arrange them in a dish, sprinkle some salt and pepper on top and add the oil and, if you wish, the parsley and garlic. Mix them lightly. Serve after a few hours. This dish may be used also as a side vegetable and mixed in with tomato salads, green salads, and raw and cooked salad (*Insalata Cruda e Cotta*, page 203).

PROSCIUTTO E MELONE

Prosciutto and Melon

Cantaloupe: 1 ripe; cut in slices. Remove the seeds and spongy
    part. Leave the rind on
Prosciutto: ¼ pound, or more, sliced very thin

Serve the cantaloupe slices along with the prosciutto, barely chilled.

    You may serve it in a different way: remove the rind from the cantaloupe, and cut the fruit into bite-size pieces. Wrap each one with a prosciutto ribbon.

INSALATA DI FAGIOLI

Bean Salad

Beans: ½ pound, dry pinto or kidney
Onion: 1 medium, cut in very small pieces. May use spring
    onion

Celery: 1 heart, leaves included, cut in very small pieces
Garlic: 1 clove, cut in minute pieces
Oregano: ½ teaspoon
Salt: 1 teaspoon
Pepper: freshly ground black, ½ teaspoon
Oil: olive, ⅓ cup

Optional:
Parsley: 2 full sprigs, cut very finely; discard the stems
Tuna: ½ cup, packed in water or oil, well drained
Vinegar: wine, 2 tablespoons

Wash and sort the beans; soak them in plenty of water (room temperature) for 12 hours. Drain and rinse the beans. Put them in a pot and add water so that it comes a few inches above them.

Add salt and bring the pot to a boil. Let the beans simmer covered until tender.

Drain them and, while still hot, mix in all the other ingredients, except the optional ones. If you have chosen to add any of the optional ingredients, wait until the beans cool. Correct the salt if necessary. Serve at room temperature a few hours after the salad has been mixed.

ZUCCA ROSSA AGRODOLCE

Sweet and Sour Squash

Note:
Do not use a cast-iron skillet to prepare this dish.

Butternut squash: 1 peeled; slice the seedless top section crosswise in ¼ inch-thick rounds. Cut the part containing the

seeds in ¼ inch-thick slices. Remove the seeds and the stringy and spongy parts.
Oil: olive, enough to cover the squash slices while frying
Vinegar: wine, ⅓ to ½ cup
Sugar: 1 tablespoon, or a little more
Garlic: 1 clove, slightly crushed in its skin
Mint: a few leaves, preferably fresh
Salt: ½ teaspoon
Pepper: freshly ground black, ½ teaspoon

Stir the sugar in the vinegar. Sprinkle salt on the squash slices; fry them over medium high heat.

After frying all the slices remove the oil from the pan. Return the squash to the pan. On high heat add the sugar-vinegar mixture, and turn the slices in the vinegar sauce for a few minutes, lifting them with a spatula so that they don't break.

Remove the squash from the heat, and place it in a glass bowl together with the sauce. Add mint, pepper, and garlic, and mix gently. It is best to let squash sit at least 2 hours before eating. Serve at room temperature.

This dish can be used also as a side vegetable.

MELANZANE SOTT'ACETO

Eggplants in Vinegar

Eggplants: 1 very fresh, slim; (see Eggplants: preparation, page 219)
Salt: to taste
Vinegar: wine
Peppers: a few small hot red chilis, dried
Pepper: freshly ground black, to taste
Garlic: 3 or 4 cloves, cut in one half, lengthwise

Peel the eggplant; cut it across in 2 sections, and slice each section lengthwise in slices a little thinner than ¼ inch. Sprinkle the eggplant evenly with salt: place it in a colander, and weigh it down (a few plates will do).

Let the eggplant drain 24 hours. Pat the slices dry, and cut them in strips a little less than a ¼ inch wide. Place them in an acid resistant container, such as glass, stainless steel, or china, and cover them with vinegar. To keep the eggplant strips from floating, place a light plate on them (you do not want to squash them). Leave the eggplant in the vinegar for 24 hours.

Have a glass jar ready, where the strips will fit closely. Remove strips from the vinegar gently with a fork, making certain they retain vinegar coating. Arrange them in layers in the jar. Follow each layer with garlic, pepper, and chili. Pour in enough oil to cover the strips. A piece of wax paper, folded over to match the size of the opening of the jar, placed on top of the oil, and thick enough to reach the rim of the jar, will keep the eggplant from floating.

Close the jar tightly, and keep in a cool place. Wait 4 weeks before eating.

POMODORI RIPIENI

Stuffed Tomatoes

Tomatoes: 6 medium size, well rounded and smooth, ripe but firm. Cut off the tops and empty them. Let them drain cut end down for 1 hour

Rice: 1 cup cooked rice, cold

Tuna: 1 cup, preserved in oil

Mayonnaise: ½ cup, (see recipe on page 74). If you don't have the time to make it, use your favorite ready-made kind

Capers: 1 tablespoon, preserved in vinegar, well drained

Parsley: 2 full sprigs, cut very finely; discard the stems
Spring onions: 2, cut in very small pieces
Pepper: freshly ground black, ¼ to ½ teaspoon

Mix together rice, tuna, mayonnaise, capers, parsley, spring onions, and pepper. Stuff tomatoes with mixture. Serve them cold.

Once the tomatoes are stuffed, they have to be served within a few hours: it is a good idea to chill the tomatoes and the stuffing separately and fill them just before serving.

POMODORI RIPIENI AL FORNO

Baked, Stuffed Tomatoes

Tomatoes: 1 or 2 per person, 3 inches across, well rounded and
    smooth: they should be firm and not overly ripe
Rice: 1½ teaspoon per tomato, Italian rice for risotti or a good
    Japanese rice
Salt: to taste
Pepper: freshly ground black, to taste
Oil: olive

Slice off and reserve tops of the tomatoes. Remove as many seeds as you can and most of the pulp being careful not to puncture the outside layer.

Choose a baking dish where the tomatoes will fit tightly, with sides approximately 2 inches high. Cover the bottom of it with a layer of oil.

Grease the tomato skins with oil, and fit them in the pan cut side up. Put in each tomato a teaspoon and a half rice, sprinkle on the rice a little salt and pepper, and trickle on it ½ teaspoon oil. Cover the tomatoes with the tops. Bake them in a 375°F preheated oven for 1 hour or until the rice is done. During the baking time remove the tomatoes from the oven, remove the tops, pour in each tomato a teaspoon of the juices collected in the pan, replace the tops, and return to the oven. Do this twice.

You may serve them hot, or room temperature. They make a very nice side dish as well.

MELANZANE RIPIENE

Stuffed Eggplants

Eggplants: 3 about 6 inches long and 3 inches across at their
    widest point
Cheese: 5 tablespoons *pecorino* (Romano), or *caciocavallo*, grat-
    ed, 3 tablespoons provolone or cheddar, coarsely grated
Salami: 3 slices, Italian, cut in very small pieces
Parsley: 3 full sprigs, cut in very small pieces, discard stems
Oil: olive
Salt: ⅓ teaspoon
Pepper: freshly ground black, ½ teaspoon
Egg: 2 small

Optional:
Tomatoes: 3 good-size tomatoes, canned, peeled, seeded, and
    cut into very small pieces

Cut off the stem end of the eggplants, then cut them in half, lengthwise. Place in a pot and fill it with water to the brim. Cover it and bring it to a boil. Let it boil 15 minutes. Drain the eggplants, and place them in a colander, cut side down for at least one hour.

Remove the pulp, being careful to leave enough attached to

the eggplant peel so that it won't collapse. Mash the pulp mixing it with 3 tablespoons *pecorino,* 3 tablespoons provolone, salami, parsley and with the salt, pepper, and eggs. Coat the skin of the eggplant halves with oil.

Choose a pan where the eggplants will fit very tightly. Coat the pan with oil, and arrange the eggplants in it. Put the filling into the halves.

If you have chosen to use the tomatoes, mix with 2 tablespoons of oil, 2 tablespoons of *pecorino,* and cover the top of the eggplants with it. Or just sprinkle the cheese on top, and trickle with oil.

Bake them in preheated 375°F oven for 45 minutes.

Serve hot.

Note:

This may be prepared in advance and warmed up for 10 minutes in the oven, preheated at 375°F.

ANTIPASTO DI CALAMARI

Squid Antipasto

Squid: 1 pound; (to clean and prepare squid see: Cleaning and Preparing Squid, page 49, and read Sea Salad, *Insalata di Mare* page 195.) Cut the hood in ½ inch rings. Separate the tentacles in groups of two or three

Lemon: juice of one

Parsley: 2 sprigs finely cut, discard the stems

Salt: ½ teaspoon

Pepper: freshly ground black, ½ teaspoon

Mix all ingredients. Refrigerate the antipasto for at least 1 hour before serving.

COZZE IN CONCHIGLIA

Mussels in the Half Shell

Mussels: 5 pounds: (to prepare, see Cleaning and Preparing
   Mussels, page 50). Remove from shells
Lemons: 5 to 6; squeeze one, slice two or three in very thin
   round slices, cut a couple in wedges
Garlic: 1 small clove, minced
Parsley: a small bunch; cut 3 sprigs very fine, keep the rest for
   decoration
Salt: to taste
Pepper: freshly ground black, to taste

Optional:
A few teaspoons of juice collected from the pan where the
mussels have been steamed open. Filter it through a sieve lined
with a fine cheese cloth.

Set aside the lemon rounds and wedges, and the parsley sprigs.
Place all the other ingredients in a bowl, mix them well, and let
them marinate in the refrigerator at least one hour.
   Select the best shells; wash and dry them well, then detach
the halves. Fill the half shells with the mussels. Depending on
how plump they are, you may use one to four mollusks. Trickle
the juice left in the bowl on the mussels.
   Arrange a little over one half of the filled shells on a plate.
Cover them with the lemon rounds, and add another layer of
shells. Top with the remaining lemon slices, and decorate the
plate with the parsley and the lemon wedges.
   Serve well chilled.

Snacks
Spuntini

MANDORLE, NOCCIOLE E NOCI INFORNATE

Oven-Roasted Nuts

Note:
Use raw, shelled nuts
Almonds: 12 minutes at 375°F
Hazelnuts: 8 to 10 minutes at 375°F
Walnuts: 8 to 10 minutes at 375°F

Preheat oven. Stir often while baking.

If almonds are to be used for dessert, reduce time to 8 minutes. If the recipe calls for crushed nuts, let them cool, then crush between sheets of waxed paper using a rolling pin; if you have a food processor, grind them, putting in a small amount at a time.

BURRO D'ACCIUGA

Anchovy Butter

Yield: ½ cup

Butter: 8 ounces, unsalted, at room temperature
Anchovies: 8 to 10, flat fillets, canned in olive oil, well drained

Cream butter and anchovies: you may do so in a food processor, by hand, or with a fork, mashing down the anchovies and the butter on a plate.

Serve slightly chilled, on slices of lightly toasted Italian or French bread.

BURRO DI TONNO

Tuna Butter

Yield: about 1½ cups

Butter: 8 ounces, unsalted
Tuna: 1 cup, packed in water, well drained
Pepper: freshly ground black, ¼ to ½ teaspoon
Salt: ½ teaspoon

If you have a food processor, puree all the ingredients together.

You may also use a hand beater, or mash the ingredients with a fork until creamy. Refrigerate. Let mixture soften some before serving. Serve with slices of slightly toasted Italian or French bread.

PÂTÉ DI OLIVE

Olive Pâté

Yield: about 1½ cups

Olives: ½ pound, Sicilian or Greek, black; pits removed
Capers: 2 tablespoons; preferably, use capers preserved in salt, well rinsed and drained. If using capers preserved in vinegar, also rinse and drain
Garlic: 2 cloves; the amount of garlic can be increased to taste
Oil: olive, 2 to 4 tablespoons

Puree in a food processor the olives, capers, and garlic. Start adding the oil in small quantities, mixing well after each addition, until the consistency of a fairly thick spread is reached.

Serve the olive pâté on slices of lightly toasted Italian or French bread.

This pâté is a very good accompaniment to rice. It may also be used as a sauce for spaghetti or linguine.

PÂTÉ DI FEGATINI DI POLLO

Chicken Liver Pâté

Yield: 1 cup

Chicken livers: 1 cup
Sage: 1 teaspoon, ground
Parsley: 2 full sprigs; discard the stems

Brandy: 1 tablespoon
Salt: ½ teaspoon
Pepper: freshly ground black, ½ teaspoon
Butter: 2 tablespoons, unsalted
Oil: olive, 1 or 2 tablespoons

Heat the butter and oil and stir-fry the chicken livers. Add sage, parsley, salt, and pepper. Keep the heat on high, and stir occasionally until all the liquid released by the livers has boiled off. Add the brandy, let it dissipate for about thirty seconds, and turn off the heat.

Let the chicken livers cool. Put it in a food processor and puree. If you don't have a food processor, you can push it through a vegetable strainer and a fine sieve. The pâté obtained by hand is finer, as no particles of membranes and fibers will go through the strainer and/or through the sieve, but it is time consuming.

Your pâté can be made creamier by adding small amounts of chicken broth to it.

Serve on toasted bread.

GAMBERI E VERDURE IN SALSA ROSA

Shrimp and Vegetables in Pink Sauce

Pink Sauce: 1½ cups; (see recipe on page 76)
Shrimp: 1 pound, medium, parboiled, shelled, well drained
Broccoli: 1 pound tips, raw
Carrots: 3 large raw, peeled, and cut into sticks

Optional:
Instead of broccoli and carrots, you may use any vegetable convenient to dip and enjoyable to eat raw; you may try also parboiled asparagus.

Arrange the shrimp and the vegetables on a plate or a tray with a bowl containing the sauce. Chill well and serve.

The tips of the shrimp and the vegetables should be dipped lightly in the sauce as they are eaten.

BURRO DI NOCI

Walnut Butter

Yield: about 2 cups

Butter: 8 ounces, unsalted at room temperature
Walnuts: 2 cups
Ham: 2 ounces, Danish

To make walnut butter it is easiest to use a food processor. Then it takes only minutes to cream all the ingredients together.

By hand use a mortar to crush the walnuts, then add the ham cut in very small pieces or ground in a grinder, and try to mash it along with the walnuts. Beat in the butter. Refrigerate.

Remove from the refrigerator a half hour before serving. Serve with slices of slightly toasted Italian or French bread.

PANZEROTTI

Filled Pastry

Yield: 10 to 11, serves 4 to 6

Crust:
(See Ricotta Cream Filled Pastry, *Cassatedde,* page 279; use same
   crust amount.)

Filling:
Ricotta: 1 cup, very well drained; (see Notes on Dairy Products,
   page 42)
Salami: 3 slices, hard Italian, cut in very small pieces
Pepper: freshly ground black, ¼ to ½ teaspoon
Salt: ½ teaspoon

Or, instead of the above filling, use:
Cheese: 3 ounces mozzarella, cut in very small pieces
   3 ounces Italian sharp cheese (fresh *caciocavallo* or provolone)
Ham: 2 ounces, cooked, cut in very small pieces
You may increase the quantity of cheese and instead of ham use
four flat anchovy fillets, preserved in oil, well drained, cut in
very small pieces.
Pepper: freshly ground black, ¼ to ½ teaspoon

Roll and divide the crust. Follow the same procedure for rolling
the crust, filling, frying, and reheating as in Ricotta Cream Filled
Pastry. The hard cheese filling is easier to fry, and the pastry
turns out a little crunchier. *Panzerotti* are usually eaten hot, but
they are also delicious at room temperature.

Sauces
Salse

BESCIAMELLA

Béchamel Sauce

Milk: 1 cup
Flour: 1½ tablespoons
Butter: 2 tablespoons unsalted
Salt: ½ teaspoon
Pepper: freshly ground black, to taste

Put flour in a small saucepan. Add a little milk, stirring with a wooden spoon until a smooth paste is formed. Keep adding small quantities of milk and stirring, thinning the mixture until smooth. Add the rest of the milk, butter, salt, and pepper. Place on a medium-low heat and stir evenly, always in one direction, until the sauce thickens (close to the boiling point). Stir down to the bottom, from the center to the sides, and from the sides to the center. If the sauce looks too thick, as you stir add more cold milk to thin it, until it reaches the desired consistency.

73

MAIONESE

Mayonnaise

Egg yolks: 5 at room temperature
Oil: 1 cup, olive at room temperature, 1 cup, corn at room temperature
Lemon: 2, squeezed; juice at room temperature
Salt: 2 teaspoons
Pepper: freshly ground black, ½ teaspoon

Optional:
Water, or very clear, light chicken broth at room temperature

Hand Method:
Choose a medium-size tepid bowl with a rounded bottom. Place the yolks in the bowl with the salt and mix them with a wooden spoon, moving the spoon in small quick circles, always in the same direction. When the yolk-salt mixture looks very creamy and consistent, start adding the oil in very small amounts. Keep turning the spoon in circular motions; before adding more oil make sure the quantity added has been well blended. After you have added one third of the oil at this slow pace, you can start adding the oil more rapidly. The secret to a good mayonnaise is a steady hand and patience.

Add the lemon juice alternating with the remaining two-thirds of the oil. Lemon juice will soften your sauce; oil will stiffen it. If you like thinner mayonnaise, add, after you have blended in all oil and lemon, small amounts of tepid water or broth, beating well after each addition. Add pepper, beat few more seconds, and correct the seasoning. If your sauce curdles, there is a very easy way to fix it. In a round bottom bowl place an egg yolk or a scant tablespoon of the curdled sauce and 1 teaspoon of all-purpose flour; beat the yolk, or the sauce-flour combination, with circular motions of your wooden spoon for a few minutes. Then start adding the rest of the curdled sauce, half a teaspoonful at a time, beating it in steadily. After few additions the sauce should look well blended; add larger amounts, two teaspoons at a time. When you have added all of the curdled sauce, proceed as per instructions if there is still oil and lemon juice to be added.

Counter-top mixer method: (Kitchen Aid K5A or similar mixer) Place the egg yolks and the salt in the mixing bowl. Beat with the wire beater, at speed 2, about 4 minutes. Start dribbling the oil by the teaspoon, at the rate of one teaspoon every 2 minutes.

After you have added 6 teaspoons, you can start dribbling the oil steadily in a thin stream, alternating with the lemon. Scrape the bowl often and increase the speed to 3. If the oil gets into the sauce faster than it can be absorbed, stop adding it for a while and wait until it gets well blended before you add more.

Do not worry if the mayonnaise looks clumpy; the only worry is when the egg and the oil start pulling apart and the sauce curdles. (In Italian we say *impazzisce,* that is, goes crazy.)

Adding lemon juice, or small quantities of water or broth, will make the mayonnaise look creamier. To retrieve a "crazy" mayonnaise use the same procedure as in the hand method.

SALSA ROSA

Pink Sauce

Mayonnaise: 1 cup: (see recipe page 74)
Cognac: 1 tablespoon
Worcestershire sauce: ½ to 1 teaspoon
Ketchup: 1 tablespoon

Mix all the ingredients together until well blended.
Taste and correct the seasoning if necessary.

SALSA VERDE

Green Sauce

Yield: about ¾ cup

Bread: 2 ounces white bread; weigh after removing all the crust
Capers: ½ cup, preserved in vinegar, moist with the packing
    liquid
Parsley: 4 full sprigs; discard the stems
Salt: ¼ teaspoon
Pepper: freshly ground black, ¼ teaspoon
Broth: (chicken or light beef) ¾ cup at room temperature

Optional:
Oil: olive, 1 teaspoon

With a food processor making this sauce takes only a few minutes. Put the bread in the broth; squeeze out most of the broth so that the bread is not soggy. Run all the ingredients in the food processor until they are well-mixed.

If you want to try to make the sauce by hand, cut the parsley very finely, then mash the parsley and the capers in a mortar, add the squeezed out bread, mash it in, add the other ingredients, and beat till everything is well mixed.

Serve with boiled meats, like brisket, beef tongue, or chicken; or serve with roasts. (See *Bollito Misto,* page 176.)

Toppings and Dressings
Condimenti

Dairy Toppings

Cheeses: imported or domestic, grate them in fine shreds; allow at least 1 tablespoon per person. Serve in a bowl.

Parmesan: *(Parmigiano)*	The most delicate of the cheeses used to top pasta, rice, and soups; goes well with any sauce that calls for a cheese topping. Made with cows' milk. Easily available in the imported and local kinds.
Romano: *(Pecorino)*	Strong tasting, wakes up any sauce; however, it overwhelms delicate sauces, so use it sparingly on them if parmesan is not available. Made with sheeps' milk. Easily available in the imported and domestic kinds.
Caciocavallo:	Lighter in flavor than *pecorino*, but just as sharp. Use it like *pecorino*. Made with cows' milk.
Ricotta, salted: *(Ricotta, salata)*	Used a lot in Sicily, it is very strong, very sharp, and very salty. It is best when combined with *salsa di pomodoro*, and *carrettiera*. Made with sheeps' milk.

American-made Parmesan and Romano definitely don't have the same taste and texture as the Italian kinds, especially the Parmesan. The qualities of sweetness and mellowness that make the Italian Parmesan so desirable become overpowering in the American version. One positive feature of the domestic Parmesan and Romano versus the imported ones is the lower cost. A pasta dish can make up the bulk of a meal and be delicious, satisfying, healthy, and relatively inexpensive; but if a main consideration in fixing pasta is to keep down the food budget, to top it with imported cheese would defeat the purpose.

A good compromise is to mix American-made Parmesan and Romano in equal parts. Their combination yields a far more acceptable taste than if used individually.

Non-dairy Toppings

MANDORLE BRUSTOLITE

Toasted Almonds

Almonds: enough to cover a skillet in a layer, shelled, whole, with skins on
Oil: olive, enough to coat the bottom of the skillet

Heat almonds and oil in a heavy skillet, stirring, over medium heat, until the almonds start browning and make a crackling sound. Remove them from the heat and place them on some paper towel to blot the oil.

The almonds will keep crunchy in an air-tight container. If you need them to top a dish, wait until they cool before crushing them.

PAN GRATTATO BRUSTOLITO

Toasted Bread Crumbs

Bread crumbs: 2 cups, unflavored
Oil: olive

In a ten-inch skillet, preferably of cast iron, pour enough oil to coat the bottom. Add the bread crumbs. Place the skillet on medium heat, and stir its contents quickly and constantly, around and down to the bottom. As soon as the bread crumbs turn to a warm brown color, turn off the heat, and stir for a couple more minutes.

Dressings

CONDIMENTO PER INSALATA

Salad Dressing

Oil: olive, ½ to ⅔ cup
Vinegar: wine, ⅓ cup
Salt: 1 teaspoon
Pepper: freshly ground black, ½ teaspoon
Oregano: 1 teaspoon

Mix all ingredients in a glass jar; unrefrigerated, it keeps for several days without losing quality.

CONDIMENTO PER INSALATA ALLA MOSTARDA

Mustard Dressing

To salad dressing above add:
Mustard: 1 teaspoon, Dijon
Garlic: 1 clove, crushed in peel

Mix all ingredients in a glass jar; it is best if you wait 1 hour before using it. Unrefrigerated, it keeps for several days.

CONDIMENTO PER INSALATA ALLA PANNA E ALL'AGLIO

Cream and Garlic Dressing

Oil: olive, ¼ cup
Cream: 2 to 3 tablespoons
Garlic: 1 clove, crushed in peel
Salt: ½ teaspoon or more
Pepper: freshly ground black, ½ teaspoon

Mix ingredients shortly before you wish to use it. As this doesn't keep, mix only the amount you are going to use.

SALMORIGANO

Salmorigano

Oil: olive, ½ cup
Lemon: ⅓ cup fresh juice
Salt: 1 teaspoon or to taste
Pepper: freshly ground black, ½ to 1 teaspoon
Oregano: 1 teaspoon

Optional:
Garlic: 1 clove, lightly crushed in its jacket
Mustard: Dijon, to taste

Mix all the ingredients. Add mustard only if you use it as salad dressing.

Use on fish, grilled meats, salads.

Lemons vary a lot in tartness and in juice content; a very tart lemon will absorb more salt than a sweeter lemon. Adjust the lemon–oil ratio and the salt to your taste.

First Courses
Primi Piatti

Doughs for Pasta

PASTA DI SEMOLA

Pasta Made with Semolina (Durum Wheat)

Semolina: 1 pound
Water: 1¼ cups; the quantity of water can vary, depending on
   the flour quality and external factors such as humidity, dry
   air, or kneading surface
Flour: unbleached, all-purpose flour
Note:
A manual machine, Atlas model 150 lusso, has been used for
rolling out and cutting. Any reference to settings has to be
applied to this machine.

Kneading the dough:
Pour the semolina in a mound on a good kneading surface. (I
like to use marble, but a butcher block or a regular formica
counter will do.) Make a well in the middle of it.

   Add about half the water to the well. Using fork or fingers,
working in a circular motion, draw the semolina closest to the
well into the water. Continue in this fashion working from the

83

inside out, drawing into the water as much flour as you can. Then start kneading, adding as much water as necessary to obtain a very stiff dough.

Knead the dough by squeezing it between your fingers and the palms of your hands, while bearing down and forward at the same time with your palms.

If you feel the dough a little too stiff to handle, dampen your hands and knead some more; repeat as needed.

As soon as the dough is smooth, cover it with a bowl turned upside down, and let it stand a few minutes.

Rolling out the dough:

Cut the dough into ten pieces. Take one, while keeping the others covered, and flatten it into a rectangle, roughly 2½ inches by 3 inches. Set the roller of your pasta machine at 1 and run the rectangle through it. Fold all the edges of the dough strip in about ½ inch, or as much as needed to give it a regular rectangular shape without raggedy edges.

Run the pasta strip again through setting 1, and put it once through settings 2 and 3. Dust it with all-purpose flour and cut it in half; it will be much easier to handle. Run the dough section through setting 4 three times and lay it on a floured surface, dust with flour spreading it evenly with your hands. *Don't* dust with flour if you are making ravioli or similar pasta. After a few minutes, run the strip 2 more times through setting 4. Cover with towels.

With every two sections you roll out stop and cut them to serve your recipe need. When a pasta strip gets too dry it is hard to put through machine cutting gear. If you are making filled pasta, edges of a too dry sheet of dough won't stick together. On the other hand, if pasta is too damp, the cutting gear won't work properly, and the strands of pasta will not separate.

Cutting fettuccine or tagliolini
(the equivalent of wide or narrow noodles):
Set the handle at the desired notch. Pick up a pasta strip and hold it perpendicularly over the machine with one of the short sides touching the cutting gear.

Start turning the handle rapidly with even circular motions. As half of the strip has gone through the machine, let go of it while still turning the handle. Catch the pasta strands from underneath to prevent them from bunching up. Lift the strips and hang them to dry.

If you do not have a pasta hanger, hang pasta to dry on the back of chair covered with towels, lightly dusted with flour. I use an old-fashioned clothes hanger that lies flat on the wall and has wooden sticks that pull out and spread around like a fan.

If you have to interrupt working with pasta, make sure the uncut strips are covered so that they won't crack. Also make sure the counter is well dusted with flour, so the pasta won't stick to it. Do not lay pasta strips one on top of the other, even if dusted with flour.

Watch your pasta while it dries. Pasta can dry and crack or stick very easily. Weather conditions can affect it one way or another. Lift the strands and lay them on the counter before they get too brittle. To let it dry safely wait about one-half hour.

As soon as you lift your pasta from the drier you can use it. The cooking time may be as brief as two minutes.

Note:
To cook see Commercial Pasta page 39.

PASTA ALL'UOVO

Egg Pasta

Read Pasta Made with Semolina, *Pasta di Semola*, page 83.

Flour: 1 pound unbleached, all-purpose flour, extra for dusting
Eggs: 3 extra large
Water: about ¼ cup; the quantity of water can vary, more or
    less, depending on the flour quality, on the egg size, and on
    air conditions

Kneading the dough:
Pour the flour into a mound on a good kneading surface. Make a
well in the middle of it, and put the eggs in the well.

Beat the eggs with a fork, and with the fork, start working the
flour immediately around them into the eggs.

As the egg-flour mixture gets too dry to handle, add ⅛ cup of
water, knead, and add more water in small amounts until you
get a stiff, smooth dough.

Knead using the same technique as in Pasta Made with
Semolina.

Rolling out the dough:
Use the same procedure as in Pasta Made with Semolina.

Cutting fettuccine or tagliolini
(the equivalent of wide or narrow noodles):
Use the same procedure as in Pasta Made with Semolina.

Note:
The cooking time may be as brief as two minutes. To cook read
Commercial Pasta, page 39.

SPAGHETTI ALLA CARRETTIERA

Cart Driver's Spaghetti

Yield: 6 servings

Oil: olive, ½ cup
Garlic: 6 cloves, 5 coarsely cut, 1 cut in minute pieces
Parsley: a fistful, finely cut; discard the stems
Romano: ¼ cup, grated
Parmesan: ¼ cup, grated
Pepper: freshly ground black, 1 teaspoon
Pasta: 18 ounces, spaghetti or rigatoni (to cook pasta see page 39)

Optional:
Pepper: hot red chili, ¼ to ½ teaspoon coarsely ground

Heat the oil and the coarse cut garlic in a skillet until aromatic and the garlic browns very lightly. Turn off the heat. Add the remaining garlic, the parsley, the pepper, and the red pepper if you wish.

Mix the cheeses in a bowl. Toss the pasta with the sauce and the cheese. If the pasta is not loose, add a little of the water it cooked in, and toss it some more.

Serve and eat immediately. (The simpler the sauce, the more important it is to shorten the time between the stove and the table.)

Note:

Topping available at the table: Parmesan and/or Romano cheese. The sauce has plenty of cheese in it, but some cheese lovers never have enough.

PASTA CON LE OLIVE NERE

Pasta with Black Olives

Yield: 4 servings

Olive pâté: 1½ cups; (see recipe page 69)
Dressed black olives: 15; see recipe, page 56; remove the pits
    and cut them in small pieces
Pasta: ¾ pound, any kind (to cook pasta see page 39)
May also be served with rice

Mix the olive pâté with the cut olives. Mix with the pasta; if too
thick, add a little of the cooking water.
Note:
Topping available at the table: no topping should be put on this
pasta, but it is polite to have a bowl of Parmesan or of a sharp
Italian cheese on the table for anyone who would want to try it.

SALSA DI POMODORO

Tomato Sauce

Yield: 4 servings

Tomatoes: 3 cups, peeled, canned, and drained; cut in half,
    widthwise. Remove most of the seeds while holding the
    tomatoes over a colander placed on a bowl. Keep collected
    juices. Cut in very small pieces. If you can find ripe, sweet,

and fleshy fresh tomatoes, they are preferable to the canned
ones. Make sure they are not too watery, and use 4 to 5
cups. Measure after peeling and removing the seeds. To
peel, see *Pesto Trapanese*, page 96

Oil: olive, enough to generously cover the bottom of a large
skillet

Onion: 1, very small, finely cut in small pieces

Garlic: 1 clove

Parsley: 1 full sprig, cut very finely; discard the stems, or use a
few leaves of basil

Salt: 1½ teaspoons

Pepper: freshly ground black, to taste

Pasta: ¾ pound. Although spaghetti is the great favorite, any
type of pasta will go well; fresh egg pasta will make it a very
special dish; to cook pasta see page 39. May also be used on
rice

Heat the oil with the onion and the garlic in the skillet until
aromatic. Onion will be translucent.

Remove the garlic and discard it. On high heat add the tomatoes; let them cook uncovered for a few minutes without
stirring. Add the salt and collected juice, and keep cooking the
sauce uncovered, over high heat, stirring occasionally for about
20 minutes.

Lower the heat if the sauce dries out too fast.

Turn off the heat and add the parsley, or the basil, and the
pepper. You may mix the sauce with the pasta, or in a very
Italian way, put the plain pasta in the individual rim plates and
spoon the sauce on top.

Note:

Topping available at the table: Parmesan, Romano, *caciocavallo*,
ricotta salata; any or all of these cheeses.

SPAGHETTI AL PIC PAC

Spaghetti with quickly cooked tomato sauce

Yield: 4 servings

Tomatoes: 4 cups, peeled, canned, and drained; cut in half
   widthwise. Remove as many seeds as you can, cut in very
   small pieces, and place in a colander for 10 minutes to drain
   excess juice. If you can find ripe, sweet, and fleshy fresh
   tomatoes, they are preferable to the canned ones. Make sure
   they are not too watery and use 5 to 6 cups. Measure after
   peeling and removing seeds. Let them drain as for peeled
   tomatoes. To peel, see *Pesto Trapanese,* page 96
Oil: olive, enough to be ¼ inch deep in a large skillet
Garlic: 2 cloves, cut in a few pieces
Parsley: 3 full sprigs, cut finely; discard the stems
Salt: 1½ teaspoon
Pepper: freshly ground black, to taste
Pasta: preferably spaghetti; (to cook pasta see page 39)

Heat the oil and the garlic in the skillet, or until aromatic and the
garlic starts taking some color.

On high heat add the tomatoes and the salt. Cook uncovered
without stirring for a few minutes, or until the tomatoes start
sizzling. Cook 5 more minutes, stirring when necessary to prevent the sauce from scorching. You may have to adjust the heat
and the cooking time to the size and type of pan you use. A wide
pan that conducts heat well will cook the sauce in the short time
indicated.

After you turn off the heat, add the parsley and the pepper.
Note:
Topping available at the table: preferably Romano or *caciocavallo* cheese.

PASTA CON LA RICOTTA

Pasta with Ricotta

Yield: 4 servings

Ricotta: 1¼ pound at room temperature
Parmesan: 4 tablespoons
Nutmeg: ¼ teaspoon
Pepper: freshly ground black, ¼ teaspoon
Pasta: ½ pound, shells (to cook pasta see page 39)

Mix ricotta with Parmesan, nutmeg, and pepper.
Add to pasta and mix along with a few tablespoons of pasta water.
Note:
Topping available at the table: Parmesan, Romano, *caciocavallo*, *ricotta salata*; any or all of these cheeses.

PENNE AI QUATTRO FORMAGGI

Penne with Four Cheeses

Yield: 6 servings

Fontina: 4 ounces, diced, or any mellow semisoft cheese, at room temperature

Provoletta: 4 ounces, cut in very small dices, or any mellow semisoft cheese, at room temperature

Emmenthal: 4 ounces, cut in very small dices, or any mellow semisoft cheese, at room temperature

Parmesan: 2 ounces, grated at room temperature

Béchamel sauce: 1 cup, see recipe, page 73 at room temperature

Pepper: freshly ground black, ½ teaspoon

Pasta: 18 ounces *penne; penne* looks like little tubes, 2 inches long and 1 inch across, with the ends cut off diagonally. The pasta closest to *penne* I have found in a supermarket is Mostaccioli Rigati. Or use anything similar, including rigatoni, to cook pasta see page 39)

Have the béchamel, the cheeses, and the pepper mixed on a large serving plate. Spread the mixture the length and width of the dish.

Do not add any cold water to the pasta before you drain it. Add the pasta immediately to the plate with the sauce after draining. Mix very thoroughly. Thin out the sauce with some of the cooking water.

Note:

Topping available at the table: Parmesan cheese.

MARGHERITE CON POMODORO E RICOTTA

Margherite with Tomatoes and Ricotta

Yield: 6 servings

Tomato sauce: 3 cups; see page 88
Ricotta: 1 pound
Basil: a few leaves
Pepper: freshly ground black, to taste
Pasta: 18 ounces, *margherite*, long strand pasta, about ½ inch
    wide, with one curled edge (not easily found), or *rotini*, or
    shells; (to cook pasta see page 39)

Warm the tomato sauce. Add to it the basil and the pepper and
mix in the ricotta with a spoon until the sauce has a fairly even
consistency. Leave some little clumps of ricotta intact.
    Mix with the pasta and serve.
Note:
Topping available at the table: Romano or *ricotta salata* cheese.

TRENETTE AL GORGONZOLA

Trenette with Gorgonzola

Yield: 4 servings

Gorgonzola: 4 ounces; use it only if very fresh. It should have a strong but not an unpleasant smell. Its consistency should be a little softer than that of Brie, and its taste should be similar to cream flavored blue cheese. To find a good Gorgonzola is not easy; you can substitute it with 2 ounces of blue cheese
Sour cream: ½ cup
Cream: heavy, ¾ cup
Walnuts: 3 tablespoons, whole or chopped
Basil: 4 large leaves
Parmesan: 2 ounces, grated
Pasta: ¾ pound, *trenette,* linguine, or spaghetti; (to cook pasta see page 39)

Cream together Gorgonzola, sour cream, walnuts, and basil in a food processor. Stir in ½ cup cream, and the Parmesan.
    Mix with the pasta. If the pasta is not loose add the remaining cream and/or some of the pasta water.
Note:
Topping available at the table: Parmesan cheese.

TRENETTE COL PESTO ALLA GENOVESE

Trenette with Genoa Pesto

Yield: 6 servings

Pine nuts: 5 tablespoons
Basil: a fistful if fresh; 2 tablespoons if dry
Garlic: 6 cloves. You may use as few as three for a less garlic
　　taste
Oil: olive, ¾ cup
Potato: 1 Idaho, medium-size, boiled and peeled, at room
　　temperature
Salt: 1 scant teaspoon
Pepper: freshly ground black, 1 teaspoon
Cheese: 2 ounces, Romano, grated: one half of it will be added
　　to the sauce, the rest will be made available at the table
Water: ½ cup, hot
Pasta: 18 ounces, *trenette* or linguine; homemade pasta is excep-
　　tionally good with this sauce (to cook pasta see page 39)

Pesto is a very simple sauce to prepare, and a sure success. Food
processors and blenders make its preparation a very quick operation. If you are using a food processor, grind garlic, pine
nuts, and basil with the steel blade. Just as they start forming a
paste, add the potato and run it just enough to be blended in.
Transfer the mixture to a bowl, and blend in, while turning the
mixture with a wooden spoon or beating with a fork, salt,
pepper, oil, and 1 ounce of the cheese.

　　Add the hot water and stir well.

　　If you are using a blender, mix all ingredients at the same
time, except the cheese and the hot water. Transfer the mixture
to a bowl and proceed to add the cheese and the hot water.

Pesto has been around longer than electricity. Purists still prepare it by hand, with a wooden mortar and pestle. If you don't have an electric gadget and don't want to get one, you can still enjoy the delights of pesto (and call yourself a purist too— say that the steel blades and the heat damage the aroma of the garlic). Invest a little money in a wooden mortar and pestle; Greek grocery stores generally carry them.

Follow the same steps as for the food processor. To turn the pine nuts, the garlic, and the basil into a paste, press the pestle against the bottom and the sides of the mortar, turning the pestle a bit at the same time. Mash the potato using a fork or a ricer, and add it to the paste. Add the other ingredients the same way as for the food processor method.

Note:

Topping available at the table: Romano cheese.

PESTO TRAPANESE

Pesto from Trapani

Yield: 8 servings

Tomatoes: 3 pounds, fresh, fleshy, ripe, and not watery (good luck!). Peel them after dipping them for 30 seconds in hot (not boiling) water. Cut them widthwise and remove the seeds. Remove the stem area. *Or* use about 20 large, firm, and peeled canned tomatoes. Clean out the seeds and drain the tomatoes well

Almonds: ¾ cup, blanched

Garlic: 6 cloves

Oil: olive, ½ cup

Basil: 1 cupful of leaves. If dry, 2 to 3 tablespoons

Salt: 1 to 2 teaspoons

Pepper: freshly ground black, 1 teaspoon

Pasta: 1½ pounds, spaghetti; (to cook pasta see page 39)

Process tomatoes in a blender or food processor until they are converted to very small pieces. Transfer two-thirds of the tomatoes to a bowl, leaving one third of the tomatoes in the processor or blender.

Add 1 teaspoon of salt and all the other ingredients to the processor or blender; blend. Transfer the mixture to the bowl and combine with the remaining tomatoes. Correct seasoning.
Note:
Topping available at the table: no topping should be added. As a courtesy to incorrigible cheese freaks, offer a bowl of *caciocavallo*, or of Romano and Parmesan cheese mixed in equal parts. (Romano would be too gamy, Parmesan too aromatic; either would kill the delicate taste of the sauce.) Also offer a bowl of fresh basil leaves; it might appease someone's desire to spread something extra on top of the pasta and would do more justice to the dish.

PISELLINI ALL'OLIO

Tiny Braised Peas

Yield: 4 to 6 servings

Peas: 20 ounces, frozen or tiny fresh (weigh after shelling)
Onion: 1 small, cut in minute pieces
Oil: olive, some
Butter: 2 tablespoons, unsalted
Salt: 1 teaspoon
Pepper: freshly ground black, to taste
Pasta: ¾ pound, *ditalini* or shells. Spaghetti if you are Italian!
    (To cook pasta see page 39)

If you are using frozen peas, dip them first in plenty of boiling

water, until they separate. Drain them. Choose a pan 10 inches round or larger. Cook the onion, the oil, and the butter until aromatic. Add the peas, add water to ½ inch in pan, the salt, and some pepper. Cover and simmer 5 minutes or until tender. The peas should retain their bright green color.
Note:
Topping available at the table: Parmesan, *caciocavallo*, or Romano cheese.

CONCHIGLIE CON ZUCCHINE A "TUTTO DENTRO"

Pasta Shells with Braised Zucchini

Yield: 4 servings

Zucchini: 3, slender, dark green, and crisp looking, cut in small dices
Yellow squash: 2, 6 to 7 inches long, slender, crisp looking, cut in small dices
Escarole: 6 to 8 leaves cut in small pieces. *Or* use the same amount of romaine lettuce
Onion: 1, small, finely cut in small pieces
Garlic: 1 clove, cut in a few pieces
Tomatoes: 4, peeled, seeded, and cut in small pieces; reserve the juice collected while seeding tomatoes
Oil: olive, enough to cover the bottom of a large frying pan
Salt: 1 teaspoon
Pepper: freshly ground black, ½ teaspoon
Pasta: 6 ounces shells; (to cook pasta see page 39). May also be used on rice

Cook onion and garlic in olive oil until aromatic. Add tomatoes and cook very rapidly over high heat a couple of minutes, stirring occasionally.

Add the vegetables, salt, pepper, and juice from the tomatoes.

Cook over high heat, stirring frequently, for about 4 minutes. The vegetables should still be firm. If the vegetables seem to be drying out too fast, reduce the heat.

Note:

Topping available at the table: no topping should be added. For people who can't do without cheese, offer a bowl of Parmesan or *caciocavallo.*

TRENETTE AGLI "SPARACELLI"

Trenette with Broccoli

Yield: 6 servings

Broccoli: 6 cups, blanched; include the tender part of the stems, peeled. Divide up the flower tips in small sections, and cut the stems in very small dices. Include any tender leaves. Keep some of the water the broccoli was cooked in.
Garlic: 6 cloves; 5 coarsely cut, 1 very minutely
Pepper: 2 small, dry, red hot chilies
Salt: 1 teaspoon
Tomato paste: 2 teaspoons
Anchovies: 6, flat, canned fillets, mashed in 2 tablespoons olive oil
Oil: olive, ½ to ⅔ cup
Pasta: ¾ pound *trenette* or linguine; (to cook pasta see page 39)

Heat the oil and coarse pieces of garlic in a very large skillet, until aromatic and the garlic starts taking some color.

On high heat add the broccoli and the peppers; stir until well coated with oil. Add salt and a small amount of water to moisten the vegetables; cook covered, over low heat, for 10 minutes.

Uncover, and add the tomato paste thinned with a couple of tablespoons of the broccoli water. Increase the heat to high and cook, stirring, until the vegetables are quite dry.

Turn off the heat. Remove the peppers; add the mashed anchovies and the remaining garlic. Mix well.

When you mix the pasta with the sauce, it might be necessary to add a little of the cooking water if it is too thick.

Note:

Topping available at the table: Romano cheese.

PASTA E FAGIOLI

Pasta and Beans

Yield: 4 servings

Beans: ¾ pound, dried pinto or similar, sorted, washed, and soaked overnight

Onion: 1, medium, cut in very small pieces

Oil: olive, ¼ cup

Tomato paste: 1 teaspoon

Salt: ½ teaspoon

Pepper: freshly ground black, to taste

Pasta: ¼ pound fresh *tagliolini* (thin and long pasta strips) (see Pasta Made with Semolina, page 83) broken up in small sections before cooking. Or use commercial *ditalini*, ziti, or shells. For cooking the pasta check the instructions within recipe text

Optional:

Bacon: 1 slice

Cook the onion in the oil until aromatic. Add the beans, tomato paste, salt, pepper, (bacon), and enough water to cover 2 inches above the bean level. Stir, cover, and bring the mixture to a boil. Lower the heat, and let the beans simmer until tender, up to 2 hours.

Check the water level during cooking and add hot water as necessary to keep the beans covered. When the beans are tender, remove one half of them from the pot, leaving all the liquid in. If you have added the bacon slice, remove and discard it. Bring the pot to a full boil and add the pasta; stir it a few times while it cooks. If the liquid dries too fast, and the pasta is not quite done, add some hot water. Keep in mind though that this is not going to be a soupy dish, and you want barely enough liquid in which to cook the pasta.

When the pasta is done, add to it the beans you had removed. Some people like to put the beans through a vegetable strainer before adding them to the pasta as it gives the dish a creamier consistency and takes care of any excess liquid.

Note:

Topping available at the table: Parmesan or *caciocavallo* cheese.

SALSA BIANCA

White Sauce

Yield: 8 servings

Cream: 1 cup, or more, heavy
Butter: 4 tablespoons, unsalted
Parmesan: ½ cup, grated
Pepper: freshly ground white, ¼ teaspoon
Pasta: 80 ravioli; (see recipe page 120); or 1½ pounds fresh
    fettuccine; (see *Pasta di Semola*, page 83); or *Pasta all'Uovo,*

(page 86). You may use commercial pasta also. (To cook pasta see page 39)

Optional:
Brain: 4 ounces, veal, steamed 20 minutes and mashed
Nutmeg: ¼ teaspoon

Melt the butter over low heat. Add the cream and heat it; do not let it boil. Turn off the heat, add all the other ingredients, and mix well.
Note:
Topping available at the table: Parmesan cheese.

SALSA ALLA PANNA E AI FUNGHI

Mushrooms and Cream Sauce

Yield: 6 servings

Cream: 2 cups, heavy
Milk: 1 cup
Cornstarch: 2 tablespoons
Salt: 1 teaspoon
Pepper: freshly ground black, ½ teaspoon
Mushrooms: 1 pound, sliced, sauteed briefly in olive oil in a
    heavy skillet
Pasta: 18 ounces, preferably homemade, or use linguine; (to
    cook pasta see page 39)

Using the same procedure on page 73, make a béchamel with 1 cup cream, 1 cup milk, cornstarch, pepper, and salt. Mix in the mushrooms.
  Mix with pasta and dilute with remaining cream.

Note:
Topping available at the table: Parmesan cheese.

SPAGHETTI AI PISELLI E PANNA

Spaghetti with Peas and Cream

Yield: 6 servings

Peas: 10 ounces, frozen
Onion: 1, small, cut in minute pieces
Ham: ½ pound, Danish or other cooked ham, lean, sliced thin, and cut in small pieces
Oil: olive, ¼ cup
Butter: 1 tablespoon
Cream: ¼ to ⅓ cup, heavy
Sour cream: ¾ to 1 cup
Salt: to taste
Pepper: freshly ground black, ¼ to ½ teaspoon
Pasta: 18 ounces, spaghetti, or any pasta that will look like rigatoni in a smaller scale; (to cook pasta see page 39)

Cook oil, butter, and onion in a skillet until aromatic; the onion will be translucent. On high heat add ½ cup water and bring to a boil. Add the frozen peas, cover, and cook a few minutes over medium heat. Loosen the peas with fork, making sure that the water level barely covers the peas. Keep the lid on and cook over low heat about five minutes or until the peas are tender but still have a bright-green color. Stir in ¼ cup heavy cream and ¾ cup sour cream. Add the ham and cook for few more minutes. Turn the heat off. Add some pepper and salt, if necessary. Add the rest of the cream if you want a thinner sauce.

Note:
Topping available at the table: Parmesan cheese.

SPAGHETTI ALLA MAÎTRE D'HÔTEL

Spaghetti with Maître d'Hôtel Sauce

Yield: 4 servings

Salsa di pomodoro: 1 ½ cups; (see recipe page 88); blend it
Mushrooms: ¾ pound, in thin slices
Cream: ½ cup, heavy
Butter: 4 tablespoons, unsalted
Salt: to taste
Pepper: freshly ground black, to taste
Pasta: ¾ pound, spaghetti or linguine; (to cook pasta see
    page 39)

Melt the butter in a large skillet, rapidly cooking the mushrooms
in it. Add the tomato sauce, cream, salt, and pepper. Stir well;
turn off the heat. Correct the seasoning.
Note:
Topping available at the table: Parmesan cheese.

SALSA AL CURRY

Curry Sauce

Yield: 6 servings

Pepper: 1, green, cut in very small squares
Onion: ½, medium, cut in very small pieces
Garlic: 1 clove, cut in minute pieces
Butter: 3 tablespoons, unsalted
Oil: olive, 3 tablespoons
Shrimp: 1½ pound (weigh after shelling), blanched and well
    drained if previously frozen *or*, instead of shrimp, chicken: 2
    whole breasts, braised, deboned, skinless, cut in small dices
Spices: a pinch each of nutmeg, thyme, mace, and cinnamon,
    and ⅓ teaspoon cumin, ⅔ teaspoon cardamon, ⅛ to ¼
    teaspoon cayenne pepper
Cream: 1½ cups, half-and-half, light cream, or milk
Flour: 2 tablespoons, all purpose, unbleached
Salt: 1 teaspoon
Pasta: 18 ounces, spaghetti or linguine; (to cook pasta, see page
    39) may also be used on rice; (see following recipe).

Optional:
If the sauce is used with rice, you may add:
Almonds: 2 tablespoons, blanched, slivered
Currants: 2 tablespoons

Dissolve the flour in a small amount of cream. Add the rest and
mix well. On low heat cook pepper, onion, and garlic in the
butter and the oil using a wide skillet; stir frequently. When the
onion is aromatic and the pepper has lost some of its crispness,

increase to high heat, add the shrimp or the chicken, and cook them, stirring a few minutes. Reduce the heat; add the spices and the salt.

Add the cream-flour mixture, stirring constantly until thickened. Turn off the heat. If you wish to use the almonds and the currants, add them.

Note:

Topping available at the table: no topping should be added.

RISO PER SALSA AL CURRY

Rice for Curry Sauce

Rice: 1½ cups converted rice
Butter: 3 tablespoons
Water: 3 cups, tap
Salt: ¾ teaspoon

Melt the butter in a saucepan, add the rice, and stir it until well coated. Add the water and the salt; stir, cover the pan, and bring it to a boil.

Reduce to very low heat and cook the rice, covered, until it has absorbed the water.

SPAGHETTI ALLA CARBONARA

Spaghetti Carbonara

Yield: 6 servings

Eggs: 2, whole, plus one yolk
Bacon: ½ pound, regular, cut in very small pieces; ½ pound, Canadian, cut in very small dices
Onion: 1, medium, cut in very small pieces
Butter: 6 tablespoons, unsalted
Oil: olive, 1 tablespoon
Wine: 5 tablespoons dry, white
Pepper: freshly ground black, ½ teaspoon
Parsley: 6 full sprigs, cut very finely; discard the stems
Salt: only if necessary to taste
Parmesan: 2 ounces, grated
Pasta: 18 ounces, spaghetti or rigatoni; (to cook pasta see page 39)

Beat the eggs with a fork in 12-inch-wide bowl. Set aside. Place the bacon, the onions, 4 tablespoons butter, and the oil in a medium size pan. Cook gently until the bacon fat starts melting and turns transparent.

Increase to high heat and stir until the bacon bits start turning brown. Add the wine, reduce, and turn the heat off. Add the remaining butter, pepper, and half of the parsley. Taste the sauce. Add a little salt if you think it needs it.

Cook pasta but do not add any cold water before draining. Immediately after draining the pasta, pour it into the bowl with the beaten egg and mix it rapidly from the bottom up.

Add the sauce and the cheese; mix it some more. To loosen it

up a little, you might add some of the drained water. Sprinkle
the other half of the parsley on top.

Note:

Topping available at the table: Parmesan cheese.

BOLOGNESE

Bolognese Sauce

Yield: 4 servings

Beef: ¾ pound, round, or any lean cut, put through the grinder
  once
Chicken livers: 2 ounces, cut in small pieces
Tomatoes: 8 large canned tomatoes, peeled and seeded, cut in
  small pieces; reserve juice collected seeding them
Onion: ½ medium, cut in very small pieces
Carrot: 1 medium, cut in very small pieces
Celery: 1 rib, cut in very small pieces
Oil: olive, enough to coat generously the bottom of an 8-inch
  pot
Wine: ¼ cup, dry, white
Butter: 2 tablespoons, unsalted
Salt: 1 to 1½ teaspoons
Pepper: freshly ground black, to taste
Pasta: ¾ pound, any commercial shape, very good with fresh
  fettuccine, (see Egg Pasta, page 86; to cook pasta see page
  39)

Optional:

Mushrooms: ½ ounce, dried, soaked in water about 2 hours
  and cut in small pieces (See Mushrooms, page 45)
Cream: ¼ cup, heavy

In the olive oil and butter cook the onion, carrot, and celery slowly until soft and aromatic.

Add the ground beef and the chicken livers; brown on high heat. Do not stir; rather, turn the meat with a spatula when well browned.

Add the white wine; let it reduce.

Add the tomatoes; cook over high heat, uncovered, for a few minutes.

Add the collected juice, salt, and pepper (and the mushrooms). Cook covered for about one-half hour. Uncover and check the seasoning; if too watery, let it cook at medium high heat, stirring often, until thicker.

Turn off heat. (Add the cream; mix.) Serve on any kind of pasta or on *Gnocchi di Patate;* (see recipe page 128), or on *Gnocchi di Semolino,* (see recipe page 130); or on rice.
Note:
Topping available at the table: Parmesan cheese.

RAGÚ

Meat Ragoût

Yield: 4 servings

Beef: 1 pound, round, brisket or chuck, lean, put through the grinder once. You may substitute ¼ pound beef with ¼ pound sausage or any amount of the beef with lean pork
Bacon: ½ strip
Onion: 1, very small, cut in very small pieces
Garlic: 1 clove
Oil: olive, enough to cover generously the bottom of a medium size pan
Tomato paste: 5 ounces

Water: some
Salt: 1 teaspoon
Pepper: freshly ground black, ½ teaspoon
Pasta: ¾ pound, any commercial kind. *Ragú* may be used on
   fresh fettuccine (see Egg Pasta, page 86); or *Gnocchi* (page
   128 and 129); or rice; (to cook pasta see page 39)

Place the oil, onion, bacon, and garlic in a heavy medium-size
pan. Cook until aromatic and the onion looks translucent. Increase to high heat and add the beef or beef and lean pork. Do
not stir the meat—let it brown undisturbed and turn it so that it
will brown on the other side. Let all the liquid released by the
meat evaporate. Stir the meat turning it, only when it is close to
getting scorched.

If you are using the sausage, pierce the sausage casing and let
the sausage boil in one inch of water for 15 minutes. Remove the
casing, discard the water, and brown the sausage in its own
drippings. Add it to the other meat along with the tomato paste
and enough water to barely cover the meat. Add salt and pepper, stir well to dissolve the tomato paste, cover the pot, and
bring it to a boil.

Reduce the heat and let the *ragú* simmer for 30 minutes,
stirring occasionally.
Note:
Topping available at the table: any cheese.

PASTA COL TONNO IN BIANCO

Pasta with White Tuna Sauce

Yield: 6 servings

Tuna: 12½ ounce can, packed in water, well drained
Oil: olive

Garlic: 4 cloves, three coarsely cut, one cut in minute pieces
Salt: to taste
Pepper: freshly ground black, to taste
Pasta: 18 ounces, spaghetti; (to cook pasta see page 39)

Cover the bottom of a skillet with a generous layer of oil. Add the coarsely cut garlic and heat it until aromatic. Add the tuna; cook it gently for a few minutes, stirring it often. While cooking it, add salt, if necessary. Turn off the heat, add the rest of the ingredients, mix the sauce well, taste, and correct the seasoning.
Note:
Topping available at the table: a bowl of finely cut parsley.

SPAGHETTI AI FRUTTI DI MARE

Spaghetti with Seafood

Yield: 6 servings

Mussels: 5 to 6 pounds, shelled; (to prepare see Cleaning and Preparing Mussels, page 50)
or
Shrimp: 1½ pound (weigh after shelling), blanched and well drained if previously frozen
or
Scallops: 1½ pounds
or
Lobster: 2 to 3 tails, cooked, cut in small pieces
or
A mixture of mussels, shrimp, and/or lobster. Use your judgement as to quantity needed
and
Oil: olive, ½ cup

Garlic: 4 cloves, 3 coarsely cut, 1 cut in minute pieces
Parsley: a fistful, cut very finely; discard the stems
Salt: 1 teaspoon
Pepper: freshly ground black, ½ teaspoon
Pasta: 18 ounces, spaghetti; (to cook pasta, see page 39)

Heat the oil and the coarsely cut garlic in a wide skillet until the garlic starts turning slightly darker. On high heat add the sea-food you have chosen to use and cook it briefly. Turn the heat off. Add the rest of the garlic, salt, pepper, and one half of the parsley. Mix the pasta with the sauce and sprinkle the rest of the parsley on top.
Note:
Topping availabe at the table: a bowl of finely cut parsley.

SPAGHETTI AI FRUTTI DI MARE IN SALSA ROSSA

Spaghetti with Seafood in Red Sauce

Yield: 6 servings

Tomato sauce: 2½ cups (see page 88) use parsley in preparation
Shrimp: 1½ pounds (weigh after shelling) blanched and well drained if previously frozen
or
Mussels: 5 to 6 pounds, shelled; (to prepare see Cleaning and Preparing Mussels, page 50)
or
Scallops: 1½ pounds
or
Lobster: 2 to 3 tails, cooked, cut in small pieces
and
Oil: olive
Garlic: 1 clove, cut in minute pieces

Parsley: 4 full sprigs, cut very finely; discard the stems
Salt: ½ to 1 teaspoon
Pepper: freshly ground black, to taste
Pasta: 18 ounces, spaghetti; (to cook pasta, see page 39)

Cover the bottom of a large skillet with a thin layer of oil. Heat and add the seafood. Cook for a few minutes on high heat. Heat the tomato sauce. Add it to the seafood; turn off the heat. Add the garlic, ½ teaspoon salt, and some pepper. Taste and correct the seasoning.

Add the parsley as soon as you mix the sauce with the pasta.
Note:
Topping available at the table: a bowl of finely cut parsley.

PASTA COL TONNO IN SALSA ROSSA

Pasta with Tuna in Red Sauce

Yield: 6 servings

Tomato sauce: 2½ cups (see *Salsa di Pomodoro*, page 88); use parsley in preparation
Tuna: 12½ ounce can, packed in water or oil, well drained
Pine nuts: 1 heaping tablespoon
Currants: 1 heaping tablespoon
Garlic: 1 clove, cut in minute pieces
Parsley: 4 full sprigs, cut very finely; discard the stems
Pepper: freshly ground black, ½ teaspoon
Pasta: 18 ounces, spaghetti or rigatoni; (to cook pasta see page 39)

Heat the tomato sauce. Add all the other ingredients except the parsley. Let the sauce stand at least 30 minutes before mixing it with pasta. Add the parsley at the same time.
Note:
Topping available at the table: a bowl of finely cut parsley.

PASTA CON L'ACCIUGA

Pasta with Anchovies

Yield: 4 servings

Tomato sauce: 2½ cups; (see *Salsa di Pomodoro,* page 88)
Anchovies: one 2 ounce can, flat fillets, well drained, mashed
Pine nuts: 1 tablespoon
Currants: 1 tablespoon
Garlic: 1 small clove, cut in minute pieces
Bread crumbs: 1 cup, toasted; (see *Pan Grattato Brustolito*
    page 80)
Pepper: freshly ground black, ½ to 1 teaspoon
Pasta: ¾ pound, spaghetti; (to cook pasta see page 39)

Heat the tomato sauce. Add the anchovies, pine nuts, currants, garlic, and pepper. Let the sauce stand for at least 30 minutes before mixing it with the pasta. Sprinkle about one fourth of the bread crumbs on top and let people help themselves to the rest at the table.
Note:
Topping available at the table: Toasted Bread Crumbs (page 88).

PASTA CON LE SARDE

Pasta with Sardines

Yield: 4 servings

Sardines: 1¼ pounds, fresh (weigh after cleaning); remove heads, tails, fins; debone. The bone is easily removed. Extend down to the tail the cut made to remove the guts; pry gently with your fingers around it and under it to expose a bone. Lift the bone from the tail up. The sardine should remain intact and open up like a butterfly

Fresh sardines are very difficult to find. As a substitute, use smelts and canned sardines as follows:

Smelts: 1 pound, fresh or frozen (use the same procedure to prepare as you would the sardines)

and

Sardines: ½ pound, canned, packed in oil, well drained. Remove the bones (do not use smoked sardines)

Anchovies: 2 ounces, canned, flat fillets, well drained, mashed

Onion: 1, small, cut in very small pieces

Fennel: a bunch of herb fennel, best if wild. As a substitute you may use the leaves from a few Florence fennels. Use the tender sprigs and only the feathery leaves of the hard sprigs. Wild fennel has a very strong aroma. Using the garden variety or the leaves from *Florence fennel* you need also ¼ teaspoon fennel seeds. If no kind of fennel leaf is available, use ½ teaspoon seeds

Oil: olive, enough to cover generously the bottom of a skillet

Salt: to taste

Pepper: freshly ground black, to taste

Almonds: ½ cup, toasted and crushed; (see Toasted Almonds, page 79)

Pine nuts: 1 tablespoon, scant
Currants: 1 tablespoon, scant
Pasta: ½ pound, *bucatini* (larger spaghetti) or, easier to find,
elbow macaroni, ½ pound; (to cook pasta see page 39)

This pasta dish may sound complicated, but, in fact, it is a rather simple first course to prepare when the ingredients are readily available. The substitutions make it a little involved, but they work out very well. It is a real stronghold of Sicilian cooking and it is worth trying.

Place the oil in a skillet, add the onion, and let it cook until aromatic and tender.

Lay the sardines or the smelts in the skillet (if you are using canned sardines, wait to add them) and sprinkle a little bit of pepper on them. If you haven't found the wild herb fennel, sprinkle ¼ teaspoon of fennel seeds on the fish, cover, and cook on low heat 8 to 10 minutes. After a few minutes of cooking, add the pine nuts and the currants, and with a spatula, turn the fish gently; cover and finish cooking. Turn off the heat and add the anchovies. If you are not using fresh sardines and are substituting, add the canned sardines at this point as well. Taste and add salt if necessary. If you are using wild herb fennel, fill a good size pot with water, add some salt, the fennel, and bring it to a boil. Cook the fennel until tender; drain it, and reserve the water.

Cut the fennel in very small pieces and add it to the cooked fish. The water you have reserved is going to be used to cook the pasta. (If you haven't found any wild fennel leaves, add ¼ teaspoon fennel seeds to the cooking water for the pasta.)

Mix the pasta with half the sauce and spoon the rest on top of it. Sprinkle on some of the almonds.
Note:
Topping available at the table: Toasted Almonds, see ingredients.

TRENETTE AL SALMONE

Linguine with Salmon

Yield: 4 servings

Salmon: 6 ounces, smoked, cut in very small pieces
Butter: 4 tablespoons, unsalted
Oil: olive, 1 tablespoon
Onion: ½, very small, cut in minute pieces
Cream: 1 cup, heavy
Cognac: 3 tablespoons
Pepper: freshly ground black, ½ teaspoon
Pasta: ¾ pound, *trenette* (linguine); (to cook pasta, see page 39)

Cook the onion very slowly in the butter and the oil until tender and aromatic.

Increase to high heat and add the cognac. Let it reduce. On low heat add the cream and the pepper, stirring often.

Turn off the heat, add the salmon. Mix well.

This sauce should not be reheated.
Note:
No topping should be used.

PASTA CON ARAGOSTA

Pasta with Lobster

Yield: 4 to 6 servings

Lobster: 1, about 2½ pounds
Tomato sauce: see recipe page 88; do not use an herb; cook the
    sauce on medium to low heat to retain more juice
Vodka: ⅓ cup, preferably Russian; any other kind you might
    use must not have any flavoring
Pasta: ¾ pound, spaghetti or linguine

Dip the lobster in a pot of boiling water; let it simmer, covered, for 20 minutes. Extract the meat from the shell. Use the white meat only. Cut it in small pieces. Blend the tomato sauce, heat it, and add the vodka.

Let the sauce cook on low heat for a couple minutes while stirring.

Turn off the heat and add the lobster.

Note:

No topping should be used.

CANNELLONI

Cannelloni

Yield: 12 or more servings

Have your filling ready before you make the pasta.

Filling:
Enough to fill about 40 cannelloni
Ragú: triple the recipe for *Ragú*, page 109
Béchamel: 6 cups; (see recipe, page 73)
Mozzarella: 1¼ pounds, cut in small dices
Cheese: ½ cup, Parmesan, grated

Mix the *ragú* and béchamel well. When cool add the mozzarella and the Parmesan.

Dough:
Read *Pasta di Semola*, page 83, and *Pasta all'Uovo*, page 86. Make a dough as for *Pasta all'Uovo*. Each of the ten sections you divided the dough into should yield two dough strips, 4 to 5 inches wide, after being rolled through setting 4 for the fifth time.

Cut them into rectangles 4 inches by 5 inches. Each of the ten sections of dough should yield 4 such rectangles plus some scraps. Set the scraps aside and keep them covered. After you have rolled out and cut the last section of dough, knead the scraps together briefly and make a few more 4- by 5-inch rectangles.

Once all the cannelloni sections are ready, they should not stand too long. As soon as you have cut the last ones, uncover them and let them dry for 5 to 10 minutes, if the dough is still too moist.

Bring a large pot with plenty of salted water to a rolling boil. Put the pasta in and stir. Be careful not to break the pasta.

Cook it following the same basic principles as for regular pasta. To test for doneness you'll have to break little corners off the cannelloni. To cook pasta see page 39.

As soon as they are *al dente,* run lots of cold water in the pot and drain them.

Pour them out in two well-buttered wide dishes.

Have two large cookie sheets, also well-buttered, ready.

Put the cannelloni in one layer on the cookie sheets; leave a layer in the dishes in which they were poured.

Cannelloni put through this process will stay *al dente* and will not stick together. Now they are ready to be filled.

Assembling and baking:
Place two tablespoons of filling on each of the sections of cooked dough along the shortest width. Roll them and put them, seam down, on a buttered baking pan. The cannelloni should fit snugly together. Spread some of the filling on top.

Bake at 375°F, in a preheated oven, for about 30 minutes.

RAVIOLI

Ravioli

Yield: 8 servings

Have your filling ready before you make the pasta.

Filling:
Butter: 2 tablespoons, unsalted
Pork: 4 ounces, very lean, ground
Beef: ½ pound, lean, ground

Sweetbreads: 3 ounces steamed; see *Animelle in Padella,* page
    161; cut them in very small pieces
Escarole: 1 pound, steamed until tender; squeeze the liquid out
    until the escarole pressed together will fill three quarters of a
    cup. Cut it very finely
Bread: 2 slices, about 2 ounces, white, without the crust,
    crumbled
Parmesan: ¼ cup, grated
Eggs: 2 whole eggs, plus 1 yolk
Marjoram: ½ teaspoon, ground
Salt: ¾ teaspoon

Melt the butter in a heavy skillet; add the pork and brown.
Remove it from the pan, and in the drippings brown the beef
and the sweetbreads. If the pan is too dry, add a little more
butter.

    Mix all the ingredients together.

Dough:
Read *Pasta di Semola,* page 83, and *Pasta all'Uovo,* page 86. Make
a dough as for *Pasta all'Uovo.* The quantity of ingredients in the
recipe will yield about 80 ravioli; there is extra dough allowed for
waste.

    Each of the ten sections you divided the dough into should
yield two dough strips, 4- to 5-inches wide, after being rolled
through setting 4 for the fifth time. Do not dust your final dough
strips with flour; just cover them. Each of the ten sections of
dough should yield 8 ravioli, 1¾ inches by 2 inches.

Shaping and cooking:
As soon as you have rolled out two of the 10 dough sections,
start filling them. Lay a dough strip on a surface dusted with
flour. Line up, along the center of the dough strip, small
amounts of the filling, one rounded teaspoon each, spacing

them to allow room for cutting, about 2½ inches from the center of each mound.

Fold the dough over, to cover the filling, so that the two long edges of the strip coincide. Tap gently around the mounds to let out as much air as possible.

Run a pasta dough cutter firmly along the overlapping edge and in between the mounds to obtain 1¾-inch by 2-inch ravioli.

Put the ravioli on a surface dusted with flour and cover them. If any are opening up, press the edges together firmly. Kitchen specialty stores have all kinds of gadgets to cut ravioli. You may be able to use them more efficiently and faster than the cutting wheel.

To cook the ravioli have plenty of salted water brought to a rolling boil; put the ravioli in and stir. The ravioli will surface right away; cover the pot and bring it to a boil again. Adjust the heat and cover the pot partially, so that the water will keep boiling without running over. Stir occasionally. Ravioli can be cooked after boiling for 15 minutes. If your pasta is a little too thick, it will take longer. It could also happen that they will be done faster than in 15 minutes.

Ravioli will puff up and then shrivel down. When they do, start checking little bits of dough from the edges for doneness. Do not add cold water to the pot before draining.

To really appreciate the ravioli taste serve them with *Salsa Bianca,* see recipe page 101. You may also serve them with *Salsa di Pomodoro,* see recipe page 88, or *Salsa alla Panna e ai Funghi,* see recipe page 102.

Some friendly advice: make ravioli only if you love them dearly (as I do), if your idea of amusement is to spend hours over a dish, and/or if you are a good sport. As I mentioned before, there are gadgets that can make the process faster, provided you can make them work. I generally find them disappointing. If you are not familiar with handling pasta dough, don't start with

ravioli. Stick to fettuccine; once you breeze through this, try your hand at ravioli.
Note:
Topping available at the table: Parmesan cheese.

RISOTTO

Risotto

Yield: 6 servings

Rice: 1 pound, Arborio for *risotti,* or top quality Japanese rice
Butter: 4 tablespoons, unsalted
Oil: olive, 1 tablespoon
Onion: 1, small, finely cut in very small pieces
Broth: 16 cups, or as much as the rice will absorb until creamy but *al dente;* make the broth by boiling about 4 pounds of chicken parts along with a carrot, a few parsley sprigs, an onion, some celery ribs, and a little salt. If you wish to use the chicken for eating, pull out the breast, thighs, or drumsticks 25 minutes after the boiling point. Let the other parts boil up to 1 hour. Pour the broth through a sieve and skim it

Keep the broth simmering. In a heavy, large pot place the butter, oil, and onion. Cook the onion until aromatic and translucent; add the rice and toss it until it is well coated with fat.

Start adding the broth with enough to cover the rice. Stir continuously, keeping the heat high enough for the liquid to boil fast.

As the liquid dries out, add more broth. The *risotto* should be done in 25 to 40 minutes.

Risotto should be served immediately as standing will change its consistency from creamy to sticky.

Note:
Topping available at the table: Parmesan cheese.

RISO AI FEGATINI DI POLLO

Rice and Chicken Livers

Yield: 6 servings

Chicken livers: 1 pound
Oil: olive, to cover bottom of wide saucepan
Onion: ½, medium, finely cut in small pieces
Rice: 2 cups, converted, wild, or brown rice
Butter: 2 tablespoons
Salt: 2 teaspoons
Pepper: freshly ground black, to taste
Thyme: ½ teaspoon, ground
Sage: ½ teaspoon, ground
Water: a few cups; *or* a light broth, chicken or beef, at room
     temperature

Place the oil and the onion in a wide saucepan; cook until
aromatic. Increase to high heat, add the chicken livers, and stir
and cook until brown. Then adjust the heat so that the liquid
released evaporates. Cook uncovered and stir frequently; add
some salt and pepper. This should be done in 15 minutes.

Melt the butter in a pan, add the rice, and stir until the rice is
well coated. Add 3 cups of water, stir, cover, and bring to a boil.
Reduce to low heat. Cook covered, checking the liquid level and
doneness frequently. White rice will require the least liquid. As
needed add more water. (Rice should be dry when done. If
using wild rice or brown rice do *not* follow package instructions
for cooking time. Let the rice be slightly chewy or *al dente*.)

When the liquid is almost completely absorbed, add chicken livers, thyme, sage, and salt. Then add a little water to deglaze the pan where the chicken livers are cooked and add it to the rice.

Note:

Topping available at the table: Parmesan cheese.

RISOTTO CON FUNGHI

Risotto with Mushrooms

Yield: 6 servings

Same ingredients as *risotto*, page 123.

plus

Mushrooms: 1 cup lightly packed, dry *porcini,* soaked in water.
   To prepare them see page 32

Follow the recipe for risotto.

   When the rice is halfway done, add the mushrooms.

   For a stronger mushroom flavor add the last water the mushrooms soaked in, making sure you don't get any sand in with it.

Note:

Topping available at the table: Parmesan cheese.

RISOTTO CON CALAMARI

Risotto with Squid

Yield: 6 servings

Squid: 1½ pounds; to clean see Cleaning and Preparing Squid, page 49. Keep the ink bladder; do not cut the hood and tentacles in pieces before cooking them
Tomato sauce: 2 cups, see recipe page 88; use parsley in preparation
Garlic: 2 cloves
Oil: olive
Rice: 2 cups, converted
Salt: to taste
Pepper: freshly ground black, to taste

Heat the tomato sauce. Add the squid and cook 2 to 3 minutes. Pull the squid out; cut the hoods in ⅓-inch rings and separate the tentacles in 2 or 3 parts.

Cover the bottom of a medium pot with a thin layer of oil. Cook the garlic in the oil until aromatic; add the rice and stir until well coated. Add to the rice the tomato sauce, the ink sac, pepper, and enough water to bring the level of the liquid an inch above the rice. Bring to a boil. Cover and cook on very low heat until all the liquid is absorbed. Taste; add more water if not done and correct the seasoning. The risotto will be ready to serve when *al dente* and fairly dry. Mix in the squid as soon as you remove the rice from the heat.
Note:
Topping available at the table: finely cut parsley.

RISOTTO CON CARCIOFI

Artichoke Risotto

Yield: 4 servings

Rice: 1¼ cups, converted
Artichokes: 4 to 5, cut in thin slices; (to prepare see Artichokes: Preparation, page 214)
Onion: 1, very small, finely cut in small pieces
Tomatoes: 5, good-size, peeled, canned, cleaned and cut in small pieces; collect the juice; (see Tomato Sauce, page 88)
Oil: olive
Water: 2 cups
Salt: 1¼ teaspoon
Pepper: freshly ground black, 1 teaspoon
Parsley: 2 full sprigs, cut in very small pieces; discard the stems

Add enough oil to a medium size saucepan to be ¼-inch high.

Add the onion, cook it until aromatic. Add the tomatoes and cook over high heat for a few minutes until they sizzle. Add the juice collected while cleaning them; add the artichokes and cook for a couple of minutes, still on high heat.

Pour the rice in; stir well; add the water, salt, and pepper. Cover and let it cook on low heat until all the liquid is absorbed. Taste for doneness; if the rice is undercooked, add a little more water and cook longer.

Serve hot with the parsley sprinkled on top.
Note:
No topping should be used.

GNOCCHI DI PATATE

Potato Dumplings

Yield: 6 servings

Potatoes: 2 pounds; plus 2 or 3 extra potatoes to allow for waste. Choose small Russet potatoes. Do not peel potatoes before cooking them

Flour: as much as potatoes will absorb, unbleached, all-purpose

Egg: 1, whole, extra large

Put the potatoes in plenty of water; bring the water to a boil. Cook over medium heat until done, about 20 minutes. Do not puncture the peel while the potatoes are cooking—you want the potatoes to be as dry as possible. Using small potatoes gives you a better chance of their being done before their peel splits. Peel the potatoes and mash them (if you are using an electric gadget, wait until they cool). If the peel splits on any of the potatoes, unless the potato gets too waterlogged, you can still use it. After you have peeled it, put it in a pan, over medium heat, and turn it around for a few minutes; the excess water should dry out.

To mix the egg and the flour with the mashed potatoes, use your hands or a mixer. (I have had the best results using the Kitchen Aid K5-A.)

Mix the egg in first, then start adding the flour. The less water you have in your potatoes, the less flour you'll need to add. When ready, the dough should be like soft putty. Roll a small piece of it lightly between the palms of your hands; it shouldn't stick. Put plenty of flour on your kneading surface and make thin dough cylinders, about the size of large bread sticks. To make cylinders start with a piece of dough the size of a small egg and roll it, first between your hands then on the kneading surface. Use quick movements and very little pressure—you might have to try it a few times before you'll be able to keep the dough from sticking or sliding away without rolling.

Keep the cylinders well coated with flour. Put a few of them side by side and cut little nuggets about ¾-inch long. With your thumb gently press each nugget against any surface with small holes, such as a draining spatula or a small-hole colander. As you press down also go forward. This step gives the nuggets the typical shell shape potato gnocchi should have.

There is an easier way—cut the cylinders in ½-inch pieces. They might not be as pretty and they will not surface as fast as the shell shapes while boiling, but the taste will be the same. Keep your gnocchi well floured and away from one another.

Bring plenty of salted water to a boil (salt the water as for cooking pasta). Lay about a third of the gnocchi on a floured plate, then slide them in the water. Wait for them to surface. After they do, let them cook a few minutes. Taste them. According to the quantity of flour mixed in the dough, the cooking time will vary. Gnocchi made with smaller amounts of flour will be done in few minutes.

Pick up the gnocchi with a slotted spoon and put them in a dish. (Gnocchi can be eaten right out of the pot or they can be baked.)

Cook the rest of the gnocchi in the boiling water, following the procedure above.

Mix some sauce with the gnocchi and spoon the rest on top. Serve.

You may also bake the gnocchi, after putting them in a buttered baking dish, mixed with sauce and topped by sauce and Parmesan or mixed with plenty of Parmesan and heavy cream. Bake them at 425°F for 5 to 10 minutes.

Note:
Serve them with: heavy cream or Tomato Sauce, page 88, or
Pesto Genovese, page 95, or *Bolognese*, page 108.
Topping available at the table: Parmesan cheese, preferably

GNOCCHI DI SEMOLINO

Farina or Semolina Dumplings

Yield: 6 servings

Farina: ½ pound, quick cooking cream of wheat, ready in 2½
    minutes
Milk: 4 cups
Egg yolk: 2, extra-large
Butter: some, unsalted
Parmesan: some, grated

Bring milk to a boil in a heavy saucepan; pour the farina in a
constant stream as you stir. Keep stirring and cook on medium
to low heat, until it is thick; add and quickly stir in the egg yolks.
Cook, stirring, one more minute.

Have some oil spread on a cookie sheet. Put the mixture on it
and flatten it out to a little less than ½ inch thick with the help of
a large wet knife blade. It may help to wet your hands and
smooth the mixture out with your palms.

Let it cool. To hasten the cooling place in the refrigerator. Cut
out 1½ to 2 inch rounds with a glass or anything sharp and
circular you have on hand. Or, cut diagonally across the layer
with a knife to form diamonds. When cutting keep cleaning and
moistening your tool, because the semolina building up on it
makes cutting difficult and causes raggedy results.

Butter a baking dish and arrange gnocchi in it. Use the odd cuttings for the bottom layer and keep adding the gnocchi to form a very low pyramid. Top it with small pieces of butter and grated Parmesan. Sprinkle with pepper if you wish. Bake at 375°F for 10 to 15 minutes.

Note:

Serve them with: Tomato Sauce, page 88, or Cream and Mushroom Sauce, page 102 or Bolognese, page 108; spread the sauce on top just before serving

Topping available at the table: Parmesan cheese.

"SFINCIONE" AND PIZZA

Sicilian Pizza and Deep-Dish Pizza

Yield: 12 servings

Dough:

Enough for two 14- by 10-inch pans; will be about 1¼ inch thick when baked

Flour: 2 pounds, all-purpose, unbleached

Lard: 6 tablespoons

or

Oil: olive, 7 tablespoons

and

Salt: 1½ teaspoons

Sugar: 2½ teaspoons

Yeast: 2 tablespoons

Water: 2½ to 3 cups, tepid

Mix flour and salt, making a well in the middle. Dissolve the yeast in ½ cup tepid water together with the sugar. Pour it in the well made in the flour.

Work the flour into the water-yeast mixture, adding to it the lard or the oil and as much water as needed to make a soft dough. If you have a counter-top mixer, such as the Kitchen Aid transfer the dough to the mixing bowl and beat first at speed 1, then at speed 2 for about 8 minutes (adjust the speed as it works best). If kneading the dough by hand, beside the usual kneading movements turn the dough often, slapping it against the working surface. Knead until very smooth, about 20 minutes.

Grease well with olive oil 2 pans, 14 by 10 inches; divide the dough between them; spread it to cover the bottoms.

Smooth some olive oil on top of the dough and place the pans in a warm place that is free of drafts to rise. This should take 1¼ to 1½ hours.

The dough is now ready to be topped by either of the following toppings.

Sicilian Pizza Topping and Assembling:
Enough to cover two 14- by 10-inch pans of dough
Tomato paste: 18 ounces
Oil: olive
Onion: 1, large, finely cut in small pieces
Cheese: 8 ounces, sharp, in thin slices; (see *Panzerotti*, page 72)
Cheese: 2 cups, Romano, grated
Anchovies: 8 ounces, flat fillets, packed in oil, well drained, minced
Oregano: 2 tablespoons
Breadcrumbs: 2 cups, scant
Pepper: freshly ground black, 2 teaspoons
Water: 18 ounces

Add to a medium-size saucepan enough oil to form a ⅓- to ½-inch layer. Add onion, reserving 2 tablespoons and heat until the onion turns aromatic and starts taking some color.

Add the tomato paste and stir for about a minute over

medium high heat. Add the water; cover and cook over low heat for about 15 minutes.

Add to the anchovies some of the sauce, and mash them till pureed.

Mix all the ingredients together, except the sliced cheese.

Bake the dough in preheated 350°F oven for 10 minutes.

Take it out of the oven and spread the slices of cheese over the dough; then add an even layer of filling.

Return to the oven and bake it 20 to 30 more minutes.

Sicilians like to trickle a little oil on top of it before serving it.

Deep-Dish Pizza Topping and Assembling:
Enough to cover two 14- by 10-inch pans.
Mozzarella: 2 pounds, in thin slices
Tomatoes: 6, 1 pound cans; seeded, well drained, cut in small
    pieces. Ideally, you should use very ripe, fresh tomatoes. If
    available, seed, slice thinly and use as the peeled tomatoes.
    3 to 4 pounds should be enough to cover the pizza
    Anchovies: 3 to 4 ounces, canned, flat fillets, preferably
    packed in olive oil; drain well; cut in small pieces
Cheese: 4 ounces, sharp cheese, in thin slices; see *Panzerotti*,
    page 72
Oil: olive
Salt: 1½ to 2 teaspoons
Oregano: 2 teaspoons, leaves

Mix the tomatoes with the salt, the oregano, and ⅓ to ½ cup oil.

Bake the dough in preheated 350°F oven for 10 minutes.

Take the dough out of the oven; you must act quickly. Dot its surface with the anchovies. Cover with mozzarella and spread the tomatoes over it. Top with the sharp cheese. Trickle the drippings from the tomato mixture over the pizza. Return to the oven and bake 20 to 30 more minutes.

"GATTÓ" DI PATATE

Potato Timbale

Yield: 6 servings

Shell:
Potatoes: 5 pounds, small Russet. Allow a few extra for waste
Eggs: 2, small, whole, plus 2 yolks
Cheese: ⅔ cup, Parmesan, grated
Salt: 1 teaspoon
Butter: 2 tablespoons, unsalted
Bread crumbs: unflavored

Filling:
See recipes for Ham Filling, page 136, or *Ragú Filling,* page 137

To cook the potatoes use the same procedure as in *Gnocchi di Patate,* page 128.

Peel and mash the potatoes while still hot. For best results mash them by hand, with the appropriate tool, or put them through a ricer.

Stir in the cheese, eggs, and salt; mix well. Grease a 2½ inch-deep baking dish with some of the butter and coat it with bread crumbs. Line it up to the rim with about two thirds of the potato mixture. Pat it down with greased hands. Put the filling in so that it stays ½ inch below the rim. Cover it with the remaining potato mix. Rather than trying to spread it, make little patties of mix between your hands, and lay them on the filling until entirely covered. Tuck the edges over it and work on the surface so that the filling is fairly well sealed in.

Melt the remaining butter and brush it over the top of the

timbale. Bake in the oven preheated at 375°F for 50 minutes to 1 hour. Remove from the oven and let it stand 15 minutes before serving. Serve in the same dish you baked it in.

"GATTÓ" DI RISO

Rice Timbale

Yield: 6 servings

Shell:
Risotto: see recipe, page 123; use same quantity
Cheese: ½ cup Parmesan, grated
Eggs: 2, whole, extra-large, plus one yolk
Butter: unsalted
Bread crumbs: some

Filling:
See recipes for *Ragú* Filling, page 137, Ham Filling, page 136, and Chicken Liver Filling, page 136

While the risotto is still hot, add cheese and eggs, stirring well. Coat a baking dish with butter and bread crumbs. Pat about two thirds of the risotto on the bottom and sides of the baking dish. Fill the shell to just below the edge. Cover with remaining rice, sealing the edge all around. Do not try to spread the rice. Flatten out patties of rice between your hands and cover the filling with them. If you find that risotto sticks to your hands and it is hard to handle, dampen your hands a little bit with oil. Melt some butter, about 2 tablespoons, and brush on top of the *Gattó*. Sprinkle on top a thin layer of bread crumbs. Bake in preheated oven at 375°F for 50 minutes to 1 hour.

Let it stand out of the oven 15 minutes before serving.

RIPIENO AL PROSCIUTTO COTTO

Ham Filling

Béchamel: 2 cups; (see recipe, page 73)
Cheese: ½ cup Parmesan, grated; ½ pound mozzarella, in small dices
Ham: ½ pound, Danish or similar, in small pieces
Peas: ½ box frozen, parboiled, well drained
Pepper: freshly ground black, ½ teaspoon

Mix all ingredients together. This can also be mixed with pasta and baked in a greased dish.
   This recipe can be made ahead of time.

RIPIENO AI FEGATINI DI POLLO

Chicken Liver Filling

Béchamel: 2 cups; (see recipe, page 73)
Cheese: ½ cup Parmesan, grated
Chicken livers: 1 pound, sauteed in oil and onions, cooked as in recipe Rice and Chicken Livers, page 124
Pepper: freshly ground black, ½ teaspoon

Mix the ingredients together. Use as needed.

RIPIENO AL RAGÚ

Ragú Filling

Ragú: as per recipe *Ragú*, page 109, substitute ¼ pound beef
with ¼ pound sausage meat
Peas: 1 cup, parboiled, fresh or frozen peas
Mozzarella: ½ pound, cut in small dices
Pine nuts: 1 tablespoon
Currants: 1 tablespoon

Have the *ragú* at room temperature, add all the other ingredients, and mix well.

RIPIENO DI CARNE O POLLO IN BIANCO

Beef or White Chicken Filling

Meat: 2 cups ground beef, browned in olive oil, or 2 cups
braised chicken breast, ground
Béchamel: 3 cups; (see recipe, page 73)
Peas: 1 cup, parboiled, frozen or fresh
Cheese: ¼ cup, Parmesan, grated
Salt: to taste
Pepper: freshly ground black, to taste

Mix all ingredients.

BRIOCHE

Brioche

Yield: 10 servings

Flour: 2 cups, unbleached, all-purpose, unsifted
Yeast: 1 tablespoon, dry at room temperature
Sugar: 1 tablespoon
Butter: 10 tablespoons, room temperature, unsalted
Eggs: 4, extra-large, room temperature
Salt: 1 teaspoon
Water: ¼ cup, warm

Optional:
Cheese: ¾ cup Jarlsberg, Emmenthal, or similar, cut in small
dices

Hand Method:
Dissolve the yeast in the water, add about one quarter of the
flour, and knead well; the dough should feel fairly soft. Gather
it into a ball, place it in a bowl, cover it, and put it in a warm place
to rise. When it has almost doubled in bulk, mix the remaining
flour with the sugar and the salt. Add one egg and the butter
and knead it until smooth. Add to it the yeast ball, kneading
together until well blended. Start adding the eggs, one by one.
After each addition beat the dough very well with both hands
wide open, forcing it down on the counter and pulling it up, for
about ten minutes. The dough should become stringy and
elastic, and snap back from the counter. Gather the dough,
place it in a bowl, cover it, and put it in a warm place to rise.
When doubled in bulk, punch it down and arrange it in a
greased ring pan. If you have decided to use the cheese, mix it in

before placing it in the pan. Cover it and let it double in bulk in a warm place.

Mixer Method:

If you have a counter-top mixer (a Kitchen Aid K5-A has been used for this recipe), prepare the yeast ball as above. To add the other ingredients follow the same procedure as in the hand method, only place the ingredients in the mixing bowl. Use the dough hook to mix in the dough ball. Switch to the flat beater and beat at the lowest speed immediately after adding each egg. Increase to setting 4 as soon as the egg is blended in. Beat 2 to 3 minutes after each egg.

   The dough should string from the bowl to the beater.

   Let it rise as in hand method.

   Bake it in a 450°F preheated oven for 15 mintues.

Note:

Use brioche as a first course pouring in the hole and over it Ham Filling, page 136, Chicken Liver Filling, page 136, or Beef or White Chicken Filling, page 137. Serve hot. Brioche may also be used as bread, hot or at room temperature.

PIZZA RUSTICA

Rustic Pizza

Yield: 6 servings

Crust:

Flour: ½ pound, unbleached, all-purpose flour

Margarine or butter: 7 tablespoons, unsalted at room temperature

Egg: 1, extra-large at room temperature

Sugar: 1 tablespoon
Salt: ½ teaspoon

For the crust, mix flour, salt, and sugar. Add the margarine and the egg; squeeze and rub the ingredients together with your hands, or use a pastry wire until you can gather it in a smooth ball. Wrap it in wax paper and let it rest in a cool place for 1 hour. (You may use it immediately, but as it is very tender, it is going to be harder to handle.) Choose a baking dish—oval or rectangular—approximately 12 by 8 inches wide and 2 inches deep.

Cut two pieces of wax paper about 14 inches long. Roll the dough in between the wax paper. First roll a 6 inch round; peel the top sheet from it; pick up the bottom sheet with the dough. Turn it, dough down, on the paper just peeled off. Peel the second sheet of paper off and lay it back on the dough round. Repeat rolling and peeling, shaping the dough layer to fit the shape of your baking pan until the dough crust is a little less than ⅕ inch thick. Peel the top paper. Dust the dough with flour.

To line the baking dish pick up the short side of the wax paper the dough is still lying on and fold it over, so that the dough is doubled up. Peel the wax paper from the top half of the dough and cut the paper. Slip your hand under the wax paper the doubled up dough is on and invert it over the pan, so that the fold of the crust runs along the middle of the pan, and the remaining wax paper is on top. Insert your hand between the dough halves and peel off the wax paper from the fold up, easing the other half of the crust down on the pan at the same time.

While this procedure might sound drawn out, it is in fact, simple to do, and it is the best way to handle a fragile dough. As the dough patches up very easily, you may roll out the crust in smaller sections, if that is easier for you, and patch them together in the pan. The crust should overlap the rim of the pan.

Filling:

Ricotta: 5 cups

Escarole: 1¼ pounds, steamed, squeezed until it can be packed into a cup

Eggs: 3, extra-large

Cheese: ¼ pound, sharp Italian cheese, cut in small pieces; as to the type of cheese, see *Panzerotti*, page 72

or

½ pound, mozzarella, diced

and

Cheese: 2 tablespoons, Parmesan, or *caciocavallo*, grated

Salami: ¼ pound, cut in very small pieces

Salt: 1 teaspoon, scant

Pepper: freshly ground black, 1 teaspoon

To make the filling, reserve the white of one egg and mix all the other ingredients well.

Assembling:

To assemble the pizza, brush the bottom of the crust with the egg white (this is to make it moisture-proof); spoon in the filling.

Fold the excess dough over. Bake in a preheated oven at 375°F for 30 minutes. Reduce the heat to 325°F and bake 30 more minutes or until the filling is firm but not dry.

Serve after letting it cool for 15 minutes.

STRACCIATELLA

Egg and Broth Soup

Yield: 6 servings

Broth: 9 to 10 cups chicken broth, see Risotto recipe, page 123

Eggs: 9, extra-large, well-beaten with a fork or whisk

Parsley: 4 full sprigs, finely cut; discard the stems

Bring the broth to a full boil. Add the eggs all at once, turn heat off, and stir with wide continuous movements until the eggs are firm.

   Pour in a serving soup bowl and sprinkle the parsley on top.
Note:
Serve it along with Italian or French bread.
Topping available at the table: Parmesan cheese.

MINESTRA DI LENTICCHE

Lentil Soup

Yield: 6 to 12 servings

Lentils: 1 pound, sorted, rinsed
Carrots: 2, large, cut in small dices
Onion: 1, medium to large, cut in small pieces
Celery: 1 heart, diced
Oil: olive, enough to cover bottom of pot

Optional:
Bacon: a few slices, whole, removed before serving
or:
Ham: 2 pounds, cut in small dices
or:
Sausage: 2 pounds cooked, in enough water to cover it, about
   20 minutes. (Pierce skin before cooking.) Discard the water,
   remove the skin, and cut it in approximately ¼ inch rounds
and:
Salt: to taste
Pepper: freshly ground black, to taste

Suggestion: You may add small quantities of tomato paste or some tomato juice; a few tomatoes, canned, peeled, cut up; one or two white potatoes, in small dices; sprigs of parsley; or a bunch of escarole leaves cut up. Adding tomato in any form will make the soup sweeter.

Cook the onion, the carrots, the celery, and (the bacon) in the oil until aromatic. Add all the other ingredients (if you are using sausage, add it only when the soup is almost done) and enough water to be 3 to 4 inches above vegetable level. Bring to a boil; simmer over low heat, covered, until tender, about 1 hour. Check the water level and stir every now and then. Add water if necessary, keeping in mind the soup has to be thick.
Note:
You may cook some short pasta (to cook pasta see page 39) and mix it with the lentils. Using the ham, the sausage, and/or the pasta is going to affect the number of servings.
Topping available at the table: cheese, Parmesan, Romano, or *caciocavallo*.

MINESTRA DI FAGIOLI

Bean Soup

Yield: 8 servings

Beans: 1 pound, pinto, kidney, or similar; sorted, rinsed, soaked overnight
Sweet potatoes: 2, large, cut in large dices
Celery: a few ribs, cut in small dices
Green, leafy vegetables: spinach, endive, escarole, lettuce, a bunch of one kind or mixed, cut in large sections

Onion: 1, large, cut in small pieces
Watercress: a few sprigs, cut in small sections
or
Parsley: a few sprigs
and
Oil: olive, to cover bottom of pot generously
Salt: to taste
Pepper: freshly ground black, to taste

Place all ingredients in a heavy pot and add enough water to be about 4 inches above level of vegetables. Bring to a boil; simmer covered until beans are very tender. If water level leaves vegetables uncovered, add small quantities of water while cooking. As soon as it is done, mash the sweet potato pieces.

The soup should have very little liquid in it. One interesting way of serving it is to puree a third of it and mix it well with the rest of the soup.
Note:
Topping available at the table: cheese, any kind.

MINESTRA DI FAVA

Fava Bean Soup

Yield: 6 servings

Fava beans: 1 pound, dry; sort and rinse
Oil: olive, enough to cover bottom of pan
Fennel: a few sprigs herb fennel or a few seeds
Bay leaf: 1
Salt: to taste
Pepper: a few whole black peppercorns, to taste

Place all the ingredients in heavy pot and add enough water to cover 2 inches above the level of the fava beans. Bring to a boil and simmer over low heat, covered, until the fava beans partially disintegrate, about 45 minutes to one hour.

Stir frequently. Remove the bay leaf when fava beans are halfway done. During the cooking time check and add small quantities of water if necessary. The soup should have a very thick consistency.

MINESTRA DI CASTAGNE E CECI

Chestnut and Chick-Pea Soup

Yield: 8 servings

Chick-peas: ½ pound, dry; sort and rinse. Soak overnight
Chestnuts: ½ pound, dry, or 1 pound fresh, shelled and peeled; cut in halves
Onion: 1, medium, cut in small pieces
Oil: olive, enough to cover bottom of pot
Salt: to taste
Pepper: freshly ground black, to taste

If you use dry chestnuts, soak them two hours. Pick any particles of peel that come loose. (Dried chestnuts are available shelled and fairly well peeled.)

Place all the ingredients in a cooking pot and add water to be 4 inches above vegetable level. Bring to a boil and simmer, covered, over low heat, until chick-peas are tender, at least 2 hours.

During the cooking time check the water level, add some if necessary, keeping in mind soup has to be thick. When the chick-peas are tender, increase the heat and cook at a rolling boil, stirring for a few minutes; this will further tenderize the chick-peas.

Note:

Fresh chestnuts should be shelled while raw: to peel them, submerge them in boiling water for a few minutes.

MINESTRA DI CECI E ZUCCA ROSSA

Chick-Peas and Squash Soup

Yield: 8 servings

Chick-peas: ¾ pound, dry; clean and rinse. Soak overnight
Squash: 1, small, butternut, peeled, seeded, dice
Onion: 1, medium, cut in small pieces
Oil: olive, enough to cover bottom of pot
Salt: to taste
Pepper: freshly ground black, to taste

Place all the ingredients in a heavy pot, and add enough water to be 4 inches above vegetable level. Bring to a boil and simmer covered until the chick-peas are tender, at least 2 hours.

During the cooking time, check the water level and add water if necessary, keeping in mind soup consistency has to be thick.

When the chick-peas are tender, increase the heat and cook at a rolling boil, stirring, for a few minutes to further tenderize the chick-peas.

Second Courses
Secondi Piatti

The second course is the part of the meal subject to the hardest scrutiny. The expectation with which diners approach the first course has dwindled, and the second course is going to be judged without that great accomplice that hunger can be. There are some steps to take to make sure your second course will receive the appreciation deserved. Read the notes on meat, pages 45, and on fish and seafood, pages 47.

Hold back on second helpings of pasta. Plan to assemble your dish, or to give it the final touches, after the end of the first course. Don't rush. If prepared in advance, reheat the dish carefully.

The only filler available between the first and the second course should be some wine and good conversation. Hold back on the bread; it has spoiled many dishes.

Present your second course gloriously decorated, with looks to match its taste and smell. Complement it with a nice vegetable on the side and, now, of course, bread.

147

ARROSTO ALLA PALERMITANA

Palermo Roast Beef Slices

Yield: 6 servings

Beef: 2 pounds, very lean; weigh after trimming all the fat. Use any of the following cuts: rump, round, sirloin tip, rib, New York strip. Have the beef cut in slices ⅓-inch thick; score the very edge of the slices all around, with the tip of a sharp knife
Oil: olive
Parsley: 2 sprigs, cut finely; discard the stems
Onion: ½ very small, cut minutely
Garlic: 1 clove, small, cut minutely
Bread crumbs: 1½ to 2 cups, unflavored
Cheese: 1 tablespoon, *caciocavallo* or Romano, grated
Salt: ¼ teaspoon
Pepper: freshly ground black, ¼ teaspoon

Mix the parsley, onion, garlic, and pepper.
   Rub it in the meat slices.
   Mix the bread crumbs with the cheese and the salt.
   Coat the slices with olive oil and then with the bread crumb mixture. Broil them, setting them as close to the heat as possible. Turn them as they sizzle; take them out as soon as they sizzle again.
   You may grill the slices on top of the stove or cook them on coals.

Variation:
Instead of beef, you may use: veal or liver. You may also use beef fillet, sliced 1-inch thick.

COTOLETTE

Cutlets

Yield: 6 servings

Beef: 1½ pounds, very lean; weigh after trimming the fat. Use
   eye of round, round, or sirloin tip; have the beef cut in slices
   ¼-inch thick. Score the very edge of the slices all the way
   around with the tip of a sharp knife. Pound lightly with the
   flat part of a meat pounder
Eggs: 2, beaten with a fork
Salt: ½ teaspoon
Bread crumbs: 1½ to 2 cups, unflavored
Oil: corn or made from seeds, enough to cover the slices while
   frying
Lemon: 2, in wedges

Dip the slices in the beaten egg; coat them with the bread
crumbs, and sprinkle the salt on top.

Heat the oil and fry the cutlets over high to medium high heat
until golden brown.

Serve surrounded by lemon wedges.

Variation:
Instead of beef you may use slices of veal, pork, or turkey breast
(there will be no need to pound them). Cook the veal and the
turkey briefly over high heat. Cook the pork over high to
medium high, longer.

POLPETTE

Meat Patties

Yield: 4 servings

Beef: 1 pound, ground, lean
White bread: two large slices
Egg: 1, extra large
Wine: ¼ cup, dry, white
or
Milk: ¼ cup
and
Onion: ½, small, finely cut in small pieces
Parsley: 2 sprigs, finely cut; discard the stems
Cheese: 3 tablespoons Romano, or *caciocavallo,* grated
Salt: ½ teaspoon
Pepper: freshly ground black, ½ teaspoon
Flour: enough to coat patties
Oil: corn or made from seeds, enough to fry patties

Mix beef, bread, egg, onion, cheese, parsley, wine (or milk), salt, and pepper. Shape the beef mixture into ten to twelve round patties, about ½ inch thick. Flour lightly. Have enough heated oil in the frying vessel so that the meat patties will be covered. Add patties at medium high heat until brown; turn and brown other side; drain on paper towel.

Serve hot.

SPIEDINI AL LIMONE

Skewered Meat in Lemon Juice

Yield: 4 servings

Beef: 2 pounds, lean; weigh after trimming the fat. Use bottom
    round or eye of the round, in slices cut ⅛ inch thick. The
    slices should be about 3 inches across
Lemon: ⅓ cup juice and the peel of ½ lemon cut in very small
    pieces and 1 lemon cut in wedges
Oil: olive, ¼ cup
Salt: ½ teaspoon
Pepper: freshly ground black, ½ teaspoon

Marinate the beef slices in a mixture of the lemon juice, lemon
peel, oil, and pepper for about 10 minutes.

Fold each slice in two, and then, like an accordion, in three.

Skewer the little bundles of meat with 2 skewers rather than
only 1, running them through both ends of each bundle. This
skewering system is used in Palermo and has remarkable ad-
vantages: the elements skewered stay firmly in place, keep the
juices in, and when you turn them on the grill they don't
revolve. Pack the bundles tightly.

Broil the *spiedini,* placing them very close to the heat. Let them
cook four to five minutes on each side, or until they sizzle. You
may grill them on top of the stove, or on coals, turning them
often.

Serve them with the lemon wedges and the juice collected in
the broiler pan.

INVOLTINI

Small Meat Rolls

Yield: 8 servings

Beef: 3 pounds; weigh after trimming all fat. Use eye of the
    round cut in slices a little thinner than ¼ inch
Bread crumbs: 2 cups
Onion: 2, medium; cut ½ onion in minute pieces and separate
    the remaining onion in layers, cutting each layer lengthwise
    in ¾ inch strips
Garlic: 1 clove, cut in minute pieces.
Parsley: 4 full sprigs, cut finely; discard the stems
Cheese: 6 tablespoons, Romano, grated
Tomato paste: 1 teaspoon
Pine nuts: 1 heaping tablespoon
Currants: 1 heaping tablespoon
Bay leaf: 1 teaspoon, crushed, or 16 whole
Salt: 1½ teaspoons
Pepper: freshly ground black, 1 teaspoon
Oil: olive

Mix 1⅓ cup bread crumbs with the onion cut in very small
pieces, garlic, 5 tablespoons cheese, parsley, pine nuts, currants, salt, and pepper.

    Mix well 3 tablespoons olive oil and the tomato paste, and add
them to the bread mixture.

    Divide the filling among the slices (about 1 heaping teaspoon
each), fold two opposing sides over a little bit, and then roll each
slice, packing in the filling as you roll it.

    Place the rolls in doubled up skewers (see Skewered Meat in

Lemon Juice, page 151), placing onion strips in between, and if you have chosen to use the whole bay leaf, distribute a couple of bay leaves within five rolls. Pack the rolls tightly together.

Coat the meat with oil. If you are not using the whole leaves, sprinkle the crushed bay leaf on now.

Mix ¾ cup bread crumbs with 1 tablespoon of cheese, coat the meat with it, and place it in a low sided baking dish. Bake in a preheated 375°F oven for about 40 minutes. You may also cook on coals or broil.

SPIEDINI ALLA PALERMITANA

Palermo Skewers

Yield: 6 servings

Beef: 1½ pounds, round, lean, ground
Eggs: 3, extra-large
Bread crumbs: 2 cups or more, unflavored
Parsley: 1 full sprig, finely cut; discard the stems
Onion: 1, small, finely cut in small bits
Cheese: ½ pound, Italian sharp, sliced ½ inch thick; see *Panzerotti*, page 72.
Cheese: 2 tablespoons, Romano or *caciocavallo*, grated
Bread: a few slices, ½ inch thick, Italian or French, stale
Salt: 1 teaspoon
Pepper: freshly ground black, ½ teaspoon
Oil: corn or made from seeds, enough to cover *spiedini* while frying

Beat the eggs with a fork. Mix one half of the eggs with the beef,

¾ cup bread crumbs, parsley, onion, grated cheese, salt, and pepper until well blended.

Shape the mixture into small croquettes. Cut the cheese and the bread slices about the same size as the meat croquettes.

Place them on doubled up skewers (see Skewered Meat in Lemon Juice, page 151); alternate meat, cheese, and bread, starting and ending with meat. Pack them tightly.

Coat the skewers with the remaining egg then with the breadcrumbs.

Fry the skewers over high to medium-high heat.

Variation:
You may substitute the beef croquettes with an increased quantity of the sliced cheese, up to 1½ pounds, and insert flat fillets of anchovies in between the bread and the cheese.

BISTECCA MARINATA IN VINO ROSSO

Steak in Red Wine Marinade

Yield: 4 to 6 servings

Steak: 2, sirloin or rump, 1½ inch thick, 5 to 7 inches across; or use 4 duck breasts, whole, deboned
Juniper berries: 2 teaspoons, crushed
Thyme: 1 teaspoon, ground
Rosemary: 1 teaspoon, leaves
Bay leaf: 1 teaspoon, crushed
Pepper: freshly ground black, 1 teaspoon
Salt: 1 teaspoon, or to taste
Wine: enough to cover the meat, dry, red
Oil: olive

Put meat in an acid-resistant container where it will fit tightly. Add the spices, except the salt, and cover with the wine. Marinate overnight.

Remove the meat from the marinade. Heat a heavy skillet, add some olive oil so that the bottom of it is well coated, and brown the meat on both sides over high heat. Reduce the heat and cook it about 10 minutes longer on each side.

In the meantime boil, uncovered, the marinade, until reduced to about one third. As soon as the meat is done, strain the marinade over the meat in the skillet while it is still on the heat. Deglaze (scrape and stir meat drippings in liquid) the pan. You may add a little water if the sauce dries out too much.

Remove from the heat, slice the meat into ⅓-inch slices, arrange on a warm plate, add the salt to the sauce, and pour it over the meat.

SALTIMBOCCA

"Jump in the Mouth"

Yield: 4 servings

Beef: 1¼ pounds, lean, eye of the round; choose a small sectioned one. Have it sliced ¼ inch thick, pound it lightly with the flat part of a meat pounder. Score the sliced edges all around with the tip of a sharp knife

Ham: ¼ pound *prosciutto crudo,* sliced thin, or enough to cover the meat slices; you may substitute with Danish ham, sliced very thin

Sage: 2 leaves per beef slice, if fresh. If dry, 1 tablespoon, ground

Oil: olive, 1 tablespoon

Butter: 4 tablespoons, unsalted
Wine: ½ cup, dry, white
Salt: to taste
Pepper: freshly ground black, ¼ teaspoon

Place the sage leaves on the meat slices or rub them with the dry sage. Secure with a toothpick a slice of ham on each; the ham should be about the same size as the beef.

Heat the oil and ½ tablespoon butter in a large skillet and start cooking the *saltimbocca* over medium to high heat. Cook a few at a time, and as they get done, put them on a plate. As the pan dries out, add more butter.

After the last ones are cooked, pour the wine in the skillet over high heat, deglaze it by stirring and scraping the meat drippings in the liquid, add a little salt and the pepper, and spoon the sauce over the *saltimbocca*.

If you wish to prepare them ahead of time, follow the same procedure as in preparing ahead of time *Scaloppine al Marsala*, below.

Variation:
In place of beef, you may use turkey breast or veal.
Note:
Good *prosciutto crudo* is hard to find. If you are not sure about its quality, you are better off using Danish ham.

SCALOPPINE AL MARSALA

Scaloppine in Marsala Sauce

Yield: 4 servings

Beef: 1½ pounds, lean, eye of the round; choose a small one.

Have it sliced ¼ inch thick, then pound it lightly with the
flat part of a meat pounder. Score the edges all around with
the tip of a sharp knife
Onion: 1, large, in thin strips
Flour: ½ cup, all-purpose
Marsala: 4 to 5 tablespoons, dry; you may substitute medium
dry sherry
Water: 2 to 3 tablespoons
Salt: ½ teaspoon, scant
Pepper: freshly ground black, ½ teaspoon
Oil: olive

Lightly flour the beef slices. Heat some oil with the onion in a
large skillet until aromatic and the onions start changing color.
Push the onion to the side of the skillet, and start adding the
scaloppine, a few at a time, and cook them over medium high
heat.

Do not overcook them. As they are done, put them on top of
the onion. If you notice the onion getting too brown or the
scaloppine on top of it getting too dry, remove the onion and the
cooked meat from the pan.

Add small amounts of oil if the pan dries out too much.

When all the slices are cooked, add the Marsala and the water
to the skillet, deglaze it (scrape and stir meat drippings in liquid)
and return to it the onion and the meat. Add salt and pepper
and mix with the Marsala sauce. If you wish to prepare the
scaloppine ahead of time, after cooking all the slices do not add
the Marsala and the water to the skillet. Cover the skillet and set
it aside. Refrigerate the meat and the onion, well covered. When
you are about ready to serve, have the *scaloppine* room temperature, heat the skillet, add the Marsala and the water, deglaze,
and proceed as above.

Variation: You may use veal.

SCALOPPINE DI MAIALE AL VINO

Pork Scaloppine in Wine

Yield: 4 servings

Pork: 1½ pounds, very lean loin, boneless, in slices a little thinner than ¼ inch
Flour: ½ cup
Salt: ½ teaspoon
Pepper: freshly ground black, ½ teaspoon
Oil: olive
Butter: 2 tablespoons

Sauce:
Wine: 2 cups, dry, white
Sugar: 2 tablespoons or more
Onion: 2, spring onions, sliced
Salt: to taste
Pepper: to taste

Mix the flour with salt and pepper and coat the scaloppine with it. Put the butter in a large skillet with enough oil to cover the bottom in a thin layer. Cook the scaloppine on medium heat, removing them from the pan as they brown on both sides.

After you have cooked the scaloppine, add the wine and all the other ingredients. Cook slowly, with no lid, until the sauce is reduced to one half.

Return the scaloppine to the pan, and let them cook with the sauce, over low heat, until hot.

SCALOPPINE AL FORMAGGIO

Cheese Scaloppine

Yield: 4 servings

Beef: 1½ pounds, lean, eye of the round; choose a small one.
   Have it sliced ¼ inch thick and pound it lightly with the flat
   part of a meat pounder. Score the edges all around with the
   tip of a sharp knife
Flour: all purpose
Onion: one, small, in strips
Oil: olive
Butter: 2 tablespoons, unsalted
Cheese: as many very thin slices as necessary to cover the beef
   slices: Swiss or similar kind, such as Gruyère or Emmenthal
Wine: ½ cup, dry, white
Salt: 1 teaspoon
Pepper: freshly ground black, ½ teaspoon

Coat the meat lightly with flour.

   Cook the onion in some of the butter and enough oil to coat
the bottom of a large skillet. When the onion starts getting
darker, remove it from the pan. Start cooking the beef over high
heat, adjusting the temperature if the pan dries out too fast. As
the scaloppine are done, remove them from the pan and add
small quantities of butter and of oil as needed to cook more
slices. Keep scraping the bottom of the skillet.

   When the last of the scaloppine have been removed from the
pan, add the wine, and let it dissipate over high heat. Add salt
and pepper and return the scaloppine to the pan, turning them
in the sauce. Probably the scaloppine won't fit in one layer in the

skillet. Get another skillet, put a thin layer of oil in the bottom of it, warm it up, add some of the wine sauce, and arrange the scaloppine. Place a slice of cheese on each scaloppina. Cover them and let them cook on very low heat for five minutes or until the cheese gets soft. Top with the onion strips.

Variation: You may use veal.

MEDAGLIONI AL GROVIERA

Gruyère Medallions

Yield: 6 to 8 servings

Beef: 1½ pounds, cooked as Cutlets, (see page 149). You may use any of the other meats indicated in the recipe instead of beef
Béchamel: 2 cups, stiff; see Béchamel, page 73. To make a stiff béchamel double the amount of flour
Spinach: 2½ pounds, steamed, squeezed; it should fill two cups
Cheese: 4 tablespoons, Parmesan, grated
Cheese: as many thin slices as necessary to cover the cutlets; Gruyère, or similar kind
Ham: as many thin slices as necessary to cover the cutlets, Danish
Pepper: freshly ground black, ¼ teaspoon

Arrange the fried cutlets in an ungreased baking dish.
　　Mix the béchamel with the spinach, Parmesan, and pepper. Spoon the béchamel mixture on the cutlets; cover each mound, first with ham, then with cheese. If you are using sliced turkey

breast to make your cutlets, put a few together to make a good slice (they tend to break in sections), and place the cheese on top first, then the ham (it will help keep the cutlet sections together), and the béchamel last.

Bake in a preheated 400°F oven for 10 minutes.

ANIMELLE IN PADELLA

Sweetbreads in the Skillet

Yield: 4 servings

Sweetbreads: 1½ pounds, steamed for ½ hour
Spring onion: 2 sliced in small rounds
Parsley: 4 full sprigs, cut very finely; discard the stems
Mint: a few leaves, cut finely
Lemon: juice of 2
Salt: 1½ to 2 teaspoons
Pepper: freshly ground black, ½ to 1 teaspoon
Oil: olive
Butter: 1 tablespoon

Split the steamed sweetbread in half.

In an acid resistant bowl put lemon, onion, pepper, mint, and one half of the parsley. Add the sweetbreads and toss them well with the marinade.

Let them stand in the marinade, turning them around once in a while, for 1 hour. Remove.

Heat a thin layer of oil in a wide skillet along with the butter.

Add the sweetbreads and brown them quickly, over high heat.

Add the marinade and some salt, deglaze (scrape and stir

meat drippings in liquid) the pan, turning the sweetbreads often. Correct the seasoning.

Sprinkle with the remaining parsley and serve at once.

PEPERONI IMBOTTITI

Stuffed Peppers

Yield: 6 servings

Peppers: 6, green or red, large; cut all around stem, remove, and reserve. Clean out the seeds
Meat: 1½ pounds, ground round, or very lean other cut
Onion: ½, small, finely cut in small pieces
Tomato paste: 2 teaspoons
Cheese: 3 tablespoons, Parmesan, grated
Pine nuts: 1 tablespoon
Currants: 1 tablespoon
Salt: ½ teaspoon
Pepper: freshly ground black, 1 teaspoon
Rice: ¾ cup, cooked
Oil: olive
Egg: 1, extra-large

Cover the bottom of a skillet generously with oil, add the onion, and cook until aromatic. Add the meat and cook over very high heat until brown. Don't stir, just turn when meat starts sizzling.

Add the tomato paste and stir. Add salt, pepper, pine nuts, and currants; cook uncovered over medium high heat, stirring often, about 10 minutes.

Remove from heat; mix it with the rice and the cheese. Let cool.

Add the egg; mix well. Stuff the peppers, and close them with the stems.

Rub the outside of the peppers with oil and bake in a preheated 375°F oven for about 1 hour and 15 minutes.

CIPOLLE RIPIENE

Stuffed Onions

Yield: 6 servings or 18 filled shells

Shells:

Onions: 5, medium; remove the peels and cut in half from root to tip. Parboil them: Bring the onions and plenty of water to a boil. Cook until they begin losing their stiffness. Drain. Separate the outer layers. Reserve the core

Filling:

Beef: 1 pound, round, lean, ground
Onion: ⅓ cup, finely cut in small pieces, use the reserved cores
Béchamel: 1 cup; see recipe page 73
Cheese: 1½ ounces, Parmesan, grated
Eggs: 3, beaten with a fork
Oil: olive
Butter: 2 tablespoons, unsalted
Salt: ½ teaspoon
Pepper: freshly ground black, 1 teaspoon
Nutmeg: ¼ teaspoon

Brown the finely cut onion in 1 tablespoon olive oil and butter. Add the ground beef and brown it; do not stir it around, turn only to prevent scorching.

Have the béchamel room temperature; mix in the cheese, eggs, beef, and season it with the salt, pepper, and nutmeg. Grease a baking dish with oil, choosing one with sides not higher than 2 inches. Take the onion layers, doubling up the ones that are thin and/or smaller. (Overlap two together, not quite all the way, to make a larger shell.) Pick up the onion shells with greased hands. Divide the filling among the shells. Fit them in the pan tightly. Bake them in the oven preheated to 325°F about 45 minutes, or until brown.

Variation:
Instead of onions, or along with the onions, you may use:
Zucchini: 6 to 9; parboil them. Split them in one half, length-wise, scrape out the seed part, fill, and bake as per onions.
Eggplant: up to about eighteen slices: use good-size eggplants, cut lengthwise; (see Eggplants: preparation, page 219, and Fried Eggplant, page 220). To fill them you just spoon some filling in the middle of the slices, roll, and pack them, seam down, in the baking dish. Follow directions for baking onions.

FALSO MAGRO or "BROCIOLONE"

Stuffed Meat Roll

Yield: 8 to 10 servings

Beef: about 3 pounds, very lean. Have the butcher cut two round steaks with no membranes interrupting the grain; they should be ¾ inch thick. Have him butterfly the steaks so that you have two fairly wide, thin, layers of meat
Oil: olive

Butter: 2 tablespoons, unsalted
Wine: ⅔ cup, dry, white

Filling:
Bread: ⅓ pound white; remove the crust and crumble
Eggs: 2, extra-large
Parsley: 4 full sprigs, finely cut; discard the stems
Onion: 1, medium, cut in minute pieces
Garlic: 2 cloves, cut in minute pieces
Cheese: 4 tablespoons *caciocavallo* or Romano, grated
Cheese: 2 ounces, Italian sharp, in small dices; as to the type of
    cheese, see *Panzerotti,* page 72
Salt: ½ teaspoon
Pepper: freshly ground black, ½ to 1 teaspoon

Optional:
Salami: 1 ounce, cut in very small pieces
Eggs: 2, hard boiled, cut in small pieces

Setting aside one third of the onion, mix together all the filling
ingredients. Divide the filling between the two layers of meat,
spreading it evenly; keep it away from the edges of the meat.
Roll the meat, just tight enough not to force the filling out. Tie
the rolls all around with a string, keeping the string turns about
½ inch apart.

    Put in a pot enough oil to cover generously the bottom; add
the butter and the onion. Cook until the onion is aromatic and
translucent. Add the meat rolls and brown them over high heat
(don't get worried if some of the filling comes out). Add the
wine and deglaze the pan by scraping and stirring the drippings
in the liquid: cover. Cook over low heat, turning it every now
and then, for 1½ hours. During the cooking time, scrape the
bottom of the pan often. If there is a lot of liquid left in the pan
remove the rolls and reduce the liquid by letting it boil uncovered. Scrape the bottom of the pan often. In the meantime

remove the string. Return the rolls to the pan and coat them with the sauce. Let the *falso magro* cool some before slicing it, giving it a chance to firm up.

After you arrange the slices on a plate, spoon the sauce over them.

VITELLO TONNATO

Veal or Beef in Tuna Sauce

Yield: 8 servings

Beef: 2 pounds, eye of round, choose one small in diameter. Tie it with a string, keeping the string turns ½ inch apart. Veal available in this country is not quite the right kind, but it can be used
Carrot: 1, large
Onion: 1, large
Celery: a few ribs
Parsley: a few sprigs
Salt: 1 teaspoon
Pepper: freshly ground black, to taste
Butter: 4 tablespoons, unsalted

Sauce:
Mayonnaise: 1 cup (see recipe page 74)
Tuna: 1 cup, canned, well drained of water or oil
Anchovies: 6, flat fillets, canned, well drained
Capers: 6 tablespoons, packed in vinegar; if you use capers packed in salt, rinse well, and add a teaspoon of wine vinegar to the sauce

Place the beef in a pot with carrot, onion, celery, parsley, salt, and some pepper. Bring it to a boil; reduce the heat to low and simmer the meat covered until done, about 2 hours.

Remove the beef from broth and let it cool. Remove the string and slice in very thin slices.

Prepare the sauce, blending tuna, anchovies, and capers; fold in the mayonnaise. Arrange the beef slices in a serving dish, spreading a thin layer of sauce on each slice. Cover with a layer of sauce; decorate. Serve cold.

Note:

Garnish the plate with slices of lemon, green olives, black olives, and Italian pickled vegetables, as well as capers.

VITELLO AL BURRO

Veal in Butter

Yield: 4 servings

Veal: 1½ pounds, cut in slices ¼ inch thin, about 3 inches across
Butter: 4 tablespoons
Lemon: 1, squeezed
Salt: ½ teaspoon
Pepper: freshly ground black, to taste

Melt some butter in a heavy skillet. Cook the veal, a few slices at a time, over high heat, a couple of minutes per side. If the pan collects liquid, let it evaporate before adding more veal; add butter as necessary.

Add the lemon juice to the pan drippings, deglaze (scrape and stir meat drippings in liquid) the pan. Add the veal, salt, and pepper. Turn the slices in the sauce and remove from the heat.

SPEZZATINO DI VITELLO

Veal Stew

Yield: 4 servings

Veal: 1½ pounds, boneless, cut in 1 inch cubes
Carrots: 2, large, cut in 1 inch cubes
Potatoes: 5, Russet, small, cut in 1 inch cubes
Onion: ½ to 1, small, cut in small pieces
Parsley: 2 full sprigs, finely cut; discard the stems
Butter: 2 tablespoons, unsalted
Oil: olive
Wine: ½ cup, dry, white
Salt: 1 to 1½ teaspoons
Pepper: freshly ground black, ½ teaspoon

Cook the onion in the butter with enough oil to cover the bottom of a medium-sized pot. Add the veal and brown it over high heat. Add the wine and cook uncovered a couple of minutes; then add all the other ingredients; cover and let it simmer on very low heat 1½ hours, stirring often.

Variation:
You may use lamb.

Note:
A veal leg will do very nicely. You can use part of it for *Vitello al Burro* page 167, and the cut up pieces for the stew.

COSTOLETTE DI AGNELLONE ALLA GRIGLIA

Grilled Lamb Chops

Yield: 4 servings

Lamb chops: 8
Oil: olive
Lemon: the juice of 2 to 3
Oregano: 3 teaspoons
Salt: to taste
Pepper: freshly ground black, 1 teaspoon

Optional:
Mint: a few leaves, cut in pieces

Rub the chops with the pepper and 2 teaspoons oregano, coat them with oil, and with the juice of half a lemon. Marinate for about 1 hour, turning often in the liquid.

In a bowl mix ¼ cup oil, the juice of 1½ to 2 lemons, 1 teaspoon oregano, and some salt. Add the mint if you wish.

Roast the chops in the broiler, set very close to the heat, or on coals.

Put them on a serving plate and pour the oil mix on top.

Variation:
You may use thick slices of beef fillet, chicken, or rabbit. The chicken and the rabbit will need to cook slowly away from the heat.

AGNELLO AL FORNO

Roast Lamb

Yield: 12 servings

Lamb: 1, 8 pound leg
Oregano: 2 tablespoons, leaves
or
Rosemary leaves: 1½ tablespoons
and
Salt: 2 teaspoons
Pepper: freshly ground black, 1 teaspoon
Oil: olive

Optional:
Some onions, in their jackets, cut in half widthwise if the herb
    used is rosemary. Quantity of onions is decided by personal
    preference.

Rub the lamb with the oregano (or rosemary), salt, and pepper;
coat it with oil. If the herb used on the lamb is rosemary, put the
onions in the same pan as the lamb and sprinkle them with
rosemary.

Bake it in oven preheated to 325°F, 20 minutes per pound.

Serve it with *salmorigano* if oregano is the herb you have used.
(See *salmorigano*, page 82.) Surround it with the onion halves,
basted with oil, if you have chosen to use rosemary as the herb.

LOMBO DI MAIALE ARROSTO NEL LATTE

Pork Loin Stewed in Milk

Yield: 6 servings

Pork: 2 pounds, boneless loin roast, tied with a string; keep the
    string turns ½ inch apart
Onion: 1, small, finely cut in small bits
Carrots: 2, large, finely cut
Oil: olive, 1 tablespoon
Butter: 2 tablespoons, unsalted
Milk: enough to cover roast
Salt: 1 teaspoon or more
Pepper: freshly ground black, 1 teaspoon

Select a heavy pan where the roast will fit snugly. Heat the oil,
butter, onion, and carrots until the onion becomes translucent.
Add the pork, salt, pepper, and milk. Cover and cook over low
heat 1½ to 2 hours. Uncover, remove the pork, and increase the
heat. Reduce the liquid until thick, stirring well to the bottom of
pan.

Remove the string from the roast. Let the pork cool some
before slicing it. Cut it in thin slices. Arrange them in a serving
dish and spoon the hot sauce over the top.

LOMBO DI MAIALE AL FORNO

Oven Roasted Pork Loin

Yield: 6 servings

Pork: 2 pounds, boneless loin roast, tied with a string; keep the
  string turns ½ inch apart
Sage: 1 tablespoon, ground, dry or fresh
Rosemary: ½ to 1 tablespoon, leaves
Salt: ½ teaspoon
Pepper: freshly ground black, ½ teaspoon
Oil: olive

Rub the oil, herbs, salt, and pepper on the roast.

Place it in a low sided baking dish.

Bake in preheated oven at 375°F for 1 hour and 20 minutes to 1½
hours, brushing it often with the drippings. A loin which is less
than 2 inches in diameter requires less baking time.

Scrape the drippings from the pan.

Let the roast cool and remove the string. Slice it very thinly
and serve with the drippings on top.

You may want to make a sauce with the pan drippings. After
removing the roast, add a few tablespoons of water to the
roasting pan, cook it over low heat on top of the stove until the
water has drawn the drippings. Distribute the sauce on the pork
slices.

POLLO ALLA CAMPAGNOLA

Country-Style Chicken

Yield: 4 to 6 servings

Chicken: 1, about 3½ pounds; remove as much fat as you can, and if you wish, the skin; cut up at the joints and cut breast in half
Olives: 10, black, large, pitted, and cut in pieces.
Rosemary: 1 teaspoon, leaves
Salt: 1 teaspoon
Pepper: freshly ground black, 1 teaspoon
Capers: 2 teaspoons, preferably preserved in salt, well rinsed
Tomato sauce: 1½ cups (see recipe page 88)

Heat the sauce; add the chicken and cook briefly, turning, over high heat. Add all other ingredients, cover, and cook over low heat ½ hour, or until done. Remove the chicken and, stirring constantly, cook the sauce over high heat, until the watery content has boiled out and the sauce is reduced. Scrape the bottom of the pan often to prevent scorching. Return the chicken pieces to the pot, turning them in the sauce until hot.

Serve with something starchy to soak up the sauce (like boiled potatoes). Or you may use the sauce to top pasta, or rice. The very best thing that goes with it is *polenta*.

Polenta: ½ pound; *polenta* is the Italian version of cornmeal
Water: 3 cups
Salt: 2 teaspoons

Bring water and salt to a rolling boil. Pour in the *polenta* in a steady stream, turning it rapidly, with a heavy wooden spoon, down to the bottom of the pot, from the sides to the center and back to the sides. Reduce heat to simmering point.

Keep stirring firmly until the *polenta* is done, about 40 minutes. Pour the polenta in a pile in a large platter, make a well in the middle of it, and pour in some of the sauce. Arrange the chicken around it, and spoon the rest of the sauce over the chicken and the *polenta*.

PETTI DI POLLO AL WHISKEY

Chicken Breast in Whiskey

Yield: 6 servings

Chicken breasts: 4, whole, divided in two
Oil: olive, enough to coat bottom of large skillet in a thin layer
Onion: 1, small, finely cut in small bits
Whiskey: 3 to 4 tablespoons; you may substitute any fine brandy
Sour cream: ¾ cup
Salt: 1 teaspoon
Pepper: freshly ground black, 1 teaspoon

Heat the onion and oil in a large skillet until aromatic and translucent.

Saute the chicken; remove it from the pan. On high heat add the whiskey, deglaze the pan (scrape and stir meat drippings in liquid), and spoon in the sour cream. Add salt and pepper; stir well. Turn off the heat, return the chicken to the pan, and coat it well with the sauce.

Arrange the chicken in a greased baking pan, skin side up. Spoon the sauce over the chicken.

Bake in preheated oven at 325°F for 35 to 45 minutes.

POLLO AGRODOLCE

Sweet and Sour Chicken

Yield: 4 to 6 servings

Note:

Do not use a cast-iron skillet.

Chicken: 1 large fryer; remove the skin and the fat. Cut it up in small pieces, dividing the breast in four parts and each thigh in two. Remove the wings and the drumsticks at the joints

Celery: 1 heart, cut in small pieces; include the leaves

Onion: 1, large, cut in very small pieces

Olives: 10, green, large, pitted, and cut up in pieces

Capers: 2 tablespoons, packed in vinegar, well drained

Vinegar: ⅔ cup, wine

Sugar: 2 tablespoons

Oil: olive

Salt: ½ teaspoon, or to taste

Pepper: freshly ground black, ½ teaspoon

Almonds: ½ cup, toasted, coarsely crushed; (see Toasted Almonds, page 79)

Put enough oil in a very large skillet to cover the bottom. Heat and add the chicken; cook it over medium to high heat until golden brown. If the chicken rests in a lot of watery liquid, discard the liquid and add a little more oil. Turn the chicken often until brown. The chicken should not be done.

Remove the chicken from the skillet. Put in the onion, celery, and enough oil to cook them. When aromatic, add the chicken; have the heat on high and put in the sugar, vinegar, olives, capers, salt, and pepper. Let the vinegar evaporate, cooking for 2 to 3 minutes, turning the chicken in the sauce. Correct the seasoning, cover the skillet, and let the chicken cook until done, about 30 minutes. Turn off the heat and mix in half of the almonds.

Serve at room temperature with the remaining almonds sprinkled on top.

Note:

If you like small game, such as rabbit and quail, this is an excellent recipe for them.

BOLLITO MISTO

Mixed Boiled Dinner

Yield: 18 to 20 servings

Brisket: 2 to 5 pounds (use the larger quantity if you make use of
  only one chicken)
Tongue: 2 ½ to 3 pounds, beef
Chicken: 1 or 2, large fryers, whole (use 2 if you use the smaller
  quantity of brisket)
Sausage: 18 links, pork
Carrots: 18 large, peeled, or more
Potatoes: 18, medium, Russet, peeled, or more
Salt: to taste

Place the brisket in a pot with water, bring it to a boil, and skim the top. Add ½ to 1 ½ tablespoons salt and boil it 3 ½ hours, or until tender.

Place the tongue in a pot with water and bring it to a boil, letting it boil for 30 minutes. Discard the water, remove the thick, rough skin from the tongue with a sharp knife and return it to the pot. Fill it with water, add half a tablespoon salt, bring it to a boil, and simmer 2 ½ hours, or until tender.

Place the chicken(s) in a pot, add 1 to 1 ½ tablespoons salt, bring it to a boil, and simmer 45 minutes.

Pierce the sausage skin and boil it in plenty of water for 30 minutes. Discard the water.

Remove the chicken(s) from the pot, making sure you keep it whole, and keep it covered and warm. Add to the broth the potatoes and the carrots and boil for 20 minutes. Turn off the heat, remove the vegetables, and return the chicken(s) to the pot.

As soon as the brisket is done, add the tongue and the sausage to the same pot. Discard the water the tongue has been cooked in; if you need extra broth to cover the brisket, the tongue, and the sausage, you may add some from the chicken. Keep all the meats in the broth until ready to serve; they can be warmed up at your convenience.

As soon as you are ready to serve, return the vegetables to the same pot the chicken(s) are in and warm them up together.
Note:
To serve, place the chicken(s) in the middle of a large platter: add the brisket and the tongue sliced thin, the sausage, the potatoes, and the carrots. Serve it on individual plates with a rim to contain some of the broth. Accompany it with *Salsa Verde* (see page 76) and mustard.

CONIGLIO PORTOGHESE

Portuguese Rabbit

Yield: 4 servings

Note:
Do not use a cast-iron skillet.
Rabbit: 4 pounds, cut up. Instead of rabbit you can use a frying
    chicken with no skin or excess fat
Onion: 1, large, cut in minute pieces
Vinegar: ⅔ cup, wine
Sugar: 2 tablespoons
Almonds: ½ cup, toasted, coarsely ground (see recipe page 79)
Oil: olive
Salt: 1 teaspoon
Pepper: freshly ground black, ½ teaspoon

Cook the rabbit in a large skillet with some oil on medium to high heat until lightly browned. Remove the meat, discard the drippings, and add to the skillet a good layer of oil and the onion. Cook the onion until aromatic. Add the vinegar mixture, meat, salt, pepper, and ¼ cup almonds. Cover and cook until done, about 30 minutes. (If you are using chicken, you may serve it deboned; debone it before returning it to the pan.)

If the sauce is watery, remove the meat from the pan and reduce the liquid. Return the meat to the pan and stir it around in the thickened sauce for a few minutes. Remove from the heat.

Let it cool off and store in the refrigerator overnight.

Serve it at room temperature with the remaining almonds sprinkled on top.

GALLINELLE AGGLASSATE

Braised Cornish Game Hens

Yield: 6 servings

Cornish game hens: 4, split in half; you may use squabs instead
Onion: 1, small, cut in very small pieces
Carrots: 2, cut in very small dices
Juniper berries: 26, crushed
Oil: olive
Lard: 1 tablespoon
Wine: 1 cup, white, dry
Thyme: 1 teaspoon
Salt: 1 teaspoon
Pepper: freshly ground black, 1 teaspoon

In a large skillet heat the oil, lard, onion, and carrots. Add the hen halves, as many as will fit. Cook on both sides for a few minutes, remove from skillet, and keep adding the halves until all are browned. Adjust the heat so that the pan won't get scorched.

Add the wine and deglaze the pan by scraping and stirring the drippings in the liquid: then add all the other ingredients. Let the sauce cook covered, over very low heat, for a few minutes. Divide the sauce and hen halves between two skillets, cover, and cook over low heat until done, about 45 minutes. Turn a few times while cooking.

ANATRA AGRODOLCE

Sweet and Sour Duck

Yield: 4 to 6 servings

Flour: all-purpose
Duck: 4 breasts, skinned, deboned
Stock: 4 duck carcasses, necks, wings, gizzards, and hearts. 4 sprigs parsley, 1 teaspoon dry thyme (or a sprig if very fresh), 2 bay leaves, 2 celery [ribs], 4 cloves, some salt, enough water to cover. For heavier stock add skin from breasts
Butter: 3 tablespoons, unsalted
Lard: 1 tablespoon
Salt: to taste
Pepper: freshly ground black, 1 teaspoon
Vinegar: 1 cup, wine
Sugar: 4 tablespoons
Onion: 1, large, in very small pieces
Parsley: 2 to 3 sprigs, cut very finely; discard stems

Lightly flour the duck breasts. Bring the water and all the ingredients for the stock to a boil; boil a few minutes and skim. Let stock water simmer 1½ hours. Strain the stock then simmer until it reaches the consistency of a light glaze (the stock will be reduced in quantity).

Melt the butter and the lard in a heavy skillet (you may have to use two skillets, so divide the shortening accordingly).

Add the duck breasts and brown them, over high heat.

Reduce the heat and cook the breasts for about 10 minutes for each side. In the last few minutes of cooking, add onion and parsley. Increase the heat and add the vinegar, sugar, and some salt. Remove the breasts from the pan and slice thinly. Mix the stock with the vinegar sauce, correct seasoning, and pour over the sliced breasts.

FRITTATA CON POMODORO E BASILICO

Frittata with Tomato and Basil

Yield: 4 to 6 servings

Eggs: 8
Cheese: 3 tablespoons, Parmesan or Romano, grated
Tomatoes: 2, fresh, ripe, peeled; or canned, peeled, seeded, well drained, cut in small pieces
Basil: a few leaves, fresh, minced; or 1 teaspoon dry
Onion: ½, small, finely cut in small pieces
Salt: ¼ teaspoon
Pepper: freshly ground black, ¼ teaspoon
Oil: olive, enough to cover generously bottom of skillet

Place all the ingredients in a bowl and beat them well with a fork. Heat the oil in a medium size skillet; as soon as the oil gets very hot, pour one half of the egg mixture in, using a ladle to be sure to get ingredients settled at the bottom of the bowl.

Reduce to low heat. Cook until inserting a spatula along the sides of the *frittata* reveals a light solid crust. Turn. To test for doneness push a spatula flat on the surface; when no foamy egg mix comes out, remove from the heat and lay the *frittata* over a piece of paper towel to absorb excess oil. Tap another piece of paper towel on the top surface.

Repeat the procedure with the remaining egg mixture.

Note:
Frittata can be a very versatile way to fix eggs; instead of basil and tomatoes try one of the following: parsley and a couple of zucchini, sliced very thin; parsley and some asparagus tips, parboiled; parsley and artichokes, sliced very thin, sauteed; leftover pasta; leftover potatoes, french-fried, or boiled, in thin slices; leftover eggplant parmigiana; etc.

UOVA AI PISELLI

Eggs and Peas

Yield: 4 servings

Eggs: 8, extra-large
Braised peas: (see recipe for *Pisellini all 'Olio,* page 97); use
    quantity suggested in recipe

Divide the peas between two 10-inch skillets and bring them to a simmer.

Break 4 eggs in each skillet, cover, and simmer for about 4 minutes; when ready the egg yolks should be covered by a white film.

Serve immediately.

UOVA AL POMODORO

Eggs in Tomato Sauce

Yield: 4 servings

Eggs: 8, extra-large
Tomato sauce: (see recipe, Tomato Sauce, page 88); use 2 cups

Divide the tomato sauce between two 10-inch skillets. Bring it to a simmer. Break 4 eggs in each skillet, cover, and simmer about 4 minutes; when ready the egg yolks should be covered by a white film.
    Serve immediately.

SARDE A "LINGUATA"

Butterflied Sardines

Yield: 4 servings

Sardines: 2 pounds; (weigh after cleaning). As fresh sardines
    are very hard to find, and I don't advise you to use them
    frozen, use smelts as a substitute (smelts freeze well). Re-
    move the heads, and butterfly (see *Pasta con le Sarde*, page
    115) them, removing the central bone. Leave the tails on
Flour: ½ to 1 cup, unbleached, all-purpose
Vinegar: ½ cup, or enough to cover the fish to marinate, wine
Salt: to taste
Oil: corn or made from seeds, enough to cover the fish while
    frying

Marinate the fish in the vinegar for about 1 hour.
Remove it from the vinegar and coat it with flour.
Sprinkle some salt on it.
Heat the oil in a skillet. Fry the fish quickly over high heat.
Serve hot or cold as an antipasto.

SGOMBRO SOTT'OLIO

Mackerel in Oil

Yield: 6 servings

Mackerel: 3, about 1 ½ pounds each, cleaned, heads and tail
    fins removed
Oil: olive, ½ cup
Lemon: 2, squeeze one, cut the other in six wedges
Vinegar: 1 tablespoon, wine
Oregano: 1 teaspoon
Salt: to taste
Pepper: freshly ground black, ½ teaspoon

Place the mackerels in a pot with enough water to cover them. Add the vinegar and some salt. Cover the pot and bring it to a boil. Let it simmer 10 minutes. Turn off the heat and let the fish stand in the pot for 10 more minutes; drain it. Scrape the skin off the fish. Fillet the fish (see Notes on Fish and Seafood, page 47). Remove the remaining bones. (Mackerel has many bones other than the central bone.) Arrange the fillets in a bowl that will contain them snugly.

Mix oil, pepper, oregano, and lemon; pour the mixture over the fish. Let it stand at least 1 hour before serving or refrigerate it overnight and serve at room temperature.

Serve with lemon wedges.

SARDE AGRODOLCE

Sweet and Sour Sardines

Yield: 4 servings

Note:
Do not use a cast-iron skillet.

Sarde a Linguata, see recipe page 183; use same amount

Cipollata Sauce:
Onion: 1, large, cut in fine strips
Vinegar: ⅔ cup, wine
Sugar: 2 tablespoons
Oil: olive, ⅓ to ½ cup
Salt: 1 teaspoon
Pepper: freshly ground black, ½ teaspoon

Cook the onion in the oil until tender. Increase the heat to high and add vinegar, sugar, salt, and pepper. Evaporate the vinegar by cooking it over high heat for a couple of minutes, stirring the whole time. Mix the sardines (smelts) with the sauce.
    Serve at room temperature.

PANOTTI DI PESCE

Fish Cakes

Yield: 4 to 6 servings

Fish: 1½ cups, cooked salmon or white fish, skinned and de-
boned (see Notes on Fish and Seafood, page 47)
Zucchini: 1 ½ cups, shredded
Eggs: 2, extra-large
Parsley: 2 full sprigs, cut finely; discard the stems
Bread crumbs: ¼ cup, unflavored
Salt: ½ teaspoon
Pepper: freshly ground black, ¼ teaspoon
Flour: semolina, or unbleached, all-purpose
Oil: corn or made from seeds, enough to deep fry

Optional:
Garlic: 1 clove, in very small pieces
Lemon: 1, cut in wedges

Mix the fish with the zucchini, eggs, parsley, bread crumbs,
salt, pepper, and (garlic).
Shape the mixture into flat oval cakes the size of your palm.
Flour them.
Fry the fish cakes over high heat about 5 minutes or until
light-golden colored. Turn them once while frying.
Serve very hot (with lemon wedges).

FILETTI DI SOGLIOLA AL GRATIN

Sole Fillets au Gratin

Yield: 4 servings

Sole: 4 fillets, about 2 pounds; you may use perch, flounder, or
other white fish
Bread crumbs: 6 tablespoons, toasted (see recipe page 80)
Cheese: 3 tablespoons, Parmesan, grated

Parsley: 3 full sprigs, cut finely; discard the stems
Garlic: 1 clove, cut in minute pieces
Salt: ½ teaspoon, scant
Pepper: freshly ground black, ½ teaspoon
Oil: olive

Coat the fillets with oil and place them in a low-sided baking dish. Mix together the bread crumbs, cheese, parsley, garlic, salt, and pepper; sprinkle the mixture on the fillets.

Bake in a preheated 400°F oven for 20 minutes or until done. When done, the edges of the fillets should be slightly curled up and brown, and the crumb dressing should have a light-brown color.

Serve immediately.

PESCE AL FORNO NEL SALE

Fish Baked in Salt

Yield: 4 to 6 servings

Fish: 1, 3 to 4 pounds, rockfish, bass, bluefish, or similar kind;
    leave head and tail on
Salt: 1 pound, regular table salt

Preheat oven to 375°F. Cover the bottom of a baking dish with a layer of salt. With toothpicks pin together the stomach flaps of the fish and place on the the salt.

Cover the fish with a layer of salt from head to tail.

Bake 15 minutes per pound (if you have a fish over 6 pounds, decrease the baking time to 10 minutes per pound).

When the fish is done, the salt will have hardened into a crust. Remove it from the top of the fish while still in the baking dish.

With the help of 2 spatulas lift the fish from the pan and turn it, the cleaned side down, on a plate. Remove the rest of the salt.

Serve with *Salmorigano*, see recipe page 82, or a sauce made with olive oil, garlic, parsley, and lemon juice.

PESCE AL FORNO RIPIENO

Stuffed Baked Fish

Yield: 6 to 8 servings

Fish: 1 good-size rockfish, 4 to 5 pounds, or two smaller ones, about 2 ½ pounds each, cleaned, heads and tails on
Onion: 1, large, cut in very small pieces
Garlic: 2 cloves, cut minutely
Celery: 1 heart, cut in very small pieces
Carrot: 1, large, cut in very small pieces
Parsley: 2 full sprigs, finely cut; discard the stems
Lemon: 1, whole, if you like lemon-peel taste; or peeled, cut in thin slices
Oil: olive
Salt: to taste
Pepper: freshly ground black, to taste

Cover the botton of a skillet with a layer of oil. Add the onion, celery, and carrot; cook until aromatic.

Turn off the heat; add the parsley and the garlic.

Coat the outside of the fish with oil and sprinkle some salt and pepper on it and in the stomach cavity.

Place the fish in a baking dish and stuff it with vegetables. Put some lemon slices in a row inside the fish, letting them stick out a little bit.

Bake in preheated oven at 375°F for about 10 minutes per pound. Test for doneness as directed in Notes on Fish and Seafood, page 47.

Serve covered with lemon slices.

RUOTA DI PESCE SPADA AL FORNO

Baked Swordfish Wheel

Yield: 12 servings

Swordfish: 6 pounds, cut in one thick chunk. Choose a section
    close to the tail and a few inches thick; include the central
    bone. If that part is not available, and the fish has been
    deboned, have a quadrant cut, so that you get a good
    chunk, as thick as it is wide. If you like a richer texture, get a
    chunk in the area surrounding the stomach. Make sure the
    flesh is a pale-pink color. Keep the skin on. If you have a
    quadrant instead of a whole round, tie a string against the
    grain and give it a few turns. Not being able to have a chunk
    completely encircled by skin, the string will work as a re-
    placement for it and will keep your wheel from sprawling
Oil: olive
Salt: 1½ teaspoons
Pepper: freshly ground black, 1 teaspoon
Oregano: 2 teaspoons

Rub the fish with salt, pepper, and oregano and coat it with oil.

Cover the bottom of a low-sided baking pan with oil (*cover*, not just grease).

Bake in preheated oven at 375°F for 1 ½ hours, basting it with its own juices every now and then.

Increase the heat to 450°F and let the fish brown about 10 minutes; check it after a few minutes. If the juices in the pan are drying out too fast, and it is browning too fast, cut the heat to 425°F.

Let it rest out of the oven for 15 mintues before serving; the meat will firm up.

Serve with *Salmorigano* (see recipe page 82), or mayonnaise (see recipe page 74), or just plain lemon wedges.

SPIEDINI DI PESCE SPADA

Swordfish Skewers

Yield: 4 servings

Swordfish: 1½ pounds (weigh after trimming off most dark parts and the skin); slice ¼-inch thick. You will encounter a definite resistance from your fishmonger to comply with your request: assure him that it is very possible to slice it that thin. As you want slices about 3 inches around you might suggest that instead of cutting through a very large section of fish, he cut it first in small chunks and then slice it

Bread: 4 slices, white, fresh sandwich bread, no crust, crumbled

Egg: 1, extra-large

Onion: ½ small, cut in minute pieces

Garlic: 1 clove, cut minutely

Parsley: 2 full sprigs, cut very finely; discard the stems

Cheese: 1½ tablespoons Parmesan, grated

Cheese: 1 ounce *caciocavallo*, or other Italian sharp cheese (see *panzerotti*, page 72), cut in very small dices

Salt: ¼ teaspoon

Pepper: freshly ground black, ¼ teaspoon
Oil: olive

Mix together all the ingredients except the swordfish and oil.
Put about a teaspoon of the mixture on each slice of fish and roll
it. Place the rolls in skewers, doubling the skewers up as in
Spiedini al limone, (see recipe page 151). Coat the skewered fish
with olive oil.

Coat the bottom of a shallow baking dish with oil, place the
fish in it, and bake it in oven preheated to 375°F for about 25
minutes; or broil.

INVOLTINI DI PESCE SPADA

Swordfish rolls

Yield: 4 servings

Swordfish: 1½ pounds; (weigh after trimming all the skin and
    as many dark parts as possible). Slices should be about 3
    inches in diameter. (See *Spiedini di Pesce Spada* for cutting the
    fish, page 190)
Bread crumbs: ¾ cup
Pine nuts: 1 tablespoon, scant
Currants: 1 tablespoon, scant
Cheese: 2 tablespoons, scant, Romano, grated
Onion: ¼ small, cut in very small pieces
Garlic: 1 small clove, cut minutely
Parsley: 2 sprigs, cut finely; discard the stems
Salt: ½ teaspoon
Pepper: freshly ground black, ½ teaspoon
Oil: olive

Toast the bread crumbs as per Toasted Bread Crumbs, page 80. As the crumbs start getting darker, add the onion and the garlic; keep cooking until it is a nice golden brown.

Turn off the heat and add pine nuts, currants, cheese, parsley, salt, and pepper. Mix well; divide the filling among the fish slices, roll them, and put them in doubled up skewers (as in *Spiedini al Limone*, page 151).

Coat the fish with oil. Preheat the broiler; have your broiler pan as close to the heat source as possible. Broil the *involtini* about 4 minutes per side.

Serve with or without lemon wedges.

PESCE ALLA GHIOTTA

Glutton's Fish

Yield: 4 servings

Fish: 2 pounds, halibut or turbot, ¾ inch thick, divided in a few
  pieces. You may use thick slices of firm (but not dry) fish,
  like snapper
Potatoes: 3, medium, Russet, boiled halfway done, peeled, cut
  in very small dices
Onion: 1, small, finely cut in small pieces
Garlic: 1 clove, slightly crushed in its own skin
Tomatoes: 4 large, canned, peeled, seeded, cut in small pieces
Olives: 10 green, preferably Greek or Italian, pitted, and cut in
  pieces
Capers: 1 tablespoon, preferably preserved in salt, well rinsed,
  drained
Pine nuts: 1 tablespoon
Currants: 1 tablespoon

Salt: ¾ teaspoon, or to taste
Pepper: freshly ground black, ½ teaspoon
Oil: olive

Place enough oil in a very large skillet to cover the bottom. Add the onions and the garlic and cook until aromatic. Remove the garlic, add the tomatoes, and cook them over high heat until they sizzle.

Add the fish and all the other ingredients. Turn the heat low, cover, and simmer until done, about 20 minutes. Halfway through cooking, turn the fish with a spatula.

ZUPPA DI PESCE

Fish Soup

Yield: 8 servings

Fish head: 1, preferably of a large snapper, split in half
Halibut: 1½ pounds, ¾ to 1-inch-thick steaks, divided in a few pieces if too large; or, some slices of a large snapper cut the same way
Squid: 1 pound (read Notes on Fish and Seafood, page 47, and Cleaning and Preparing Squid, page 49). Cut the hoods in rings, ¾-inch wide, and divide the tentacles in two groups. You may use the ink sacs
Eel: 1 pound; if you'd rather not serve eel, use rockfish, including the head; the head is necessary to replace some of the richness of the eel. Have the eel cut in 3- to 4-inch sections
Mussels: 1 pound, (see Notes on Cleaning and Preparing Mussels, page 50); when steaming the mussels, remove them from the pan as soon as they open. Leave the mussels in the shell. Reserve the juice

Shrimp: ½ pound, in the shell if they are truly fresh or if they do not have any offending odor and if the shells are firmly attached; if not, use them shelled, dipped in boiling water for 30 seconds, drained, rinsed in cold water, and drained again

Onion: 1, small, cut in very small pieces

Garlic: 3 cloves, cut minutely

Tomatoes: 6, large, peeled, canned, seeded, and cut in very small pieces

Parsley: 4 full sprigs, finely cut; discard the stems

Salt: 2 teaspoons, or more

Pepper: freshly ground black, 1 teaspoon or more

Oil: olive

Wine: ½ cup, dry, white

Optional:

Saffron: ¼ teaspoon; crush the stigmas and soak them in a couple of tablespoons of the cooking liquid

or

Pesto Trapanese: 1½ cups; (see recipe page 96—do not add the basil)

Heat the oil and the onions in a very large pan. When aromatic add the halibut, the eel (or the substitutes), and the fish head, cooking briefly over high heat on both sides. Add the wine, let it evaporate, then add the tomatoes, garlic, parsley, and season with salt and pepper.

Cover the pan and let it cook on low heat a few minutes. Add about 4 cups of hot water; cover again and let it simmer 8 to 10 minutes. (If you wish to add the saffron, do so during this cooking period.)

With a spatula remove the fish from the pan and cover it so that it won't dry out. Add the squid, the shrimp, and the mussels to the broth, cooking a few minutes over high heat until the squid and the shrimp turn white. Turn off the heat.

Check the seasoning and correct if necessary. Return the halibut and the eel to the pan.

Serve with ½-inch slices of French bread, or Italian bread, quickly sauteed in a pan with olive oil.

In the Trapani area fish soup is eaten mixed with *Trapani Pesto* sauce and with *Couscous*.

Couscous is available in a very easy to cook package. Add quite a bit of black pepper to it and instead of plain water use a light chicken broth. Use a little more liquid than suggested in the instructions on the box.

Spoon the fish soup mixed with pesto on it; place the fish on the side.

INSALATA DI MARE

Sea Salad

Yield: 6 servings

Shrimp: 2 pounds, shelled, dipped in boiling water until white; drain. Rinse well in cold water if not fresh, or, if after draining shrimp retains an unpleasant smell

Squid: 1 pound, fresh or frozen, dipped in boiling water until white but still plump; drain. If squid retains an unpleasant smell, rinse it in cold water. (See Cleaning and Preparing Squid, page 49.) No ink sac needed. Cut the hoods in ⅓-inch rings and divide the tentacles in two or more groups, depending on the size of the squid

Mussels: 4 pounds, steamed open, shelled; (see Notes on Cleaning and Preparing Mussels, page 50)

Parsley: a fistful, finely cut; discard the stems

Garlic: 1 or 2 cloves, cut in minute pieces

Oil: olive, ½ cup

Lemon: 2, squeezed
Salt: 1 teaspoon or more
Pepper: freshly ground black, 1 teaspoon

Optional:
Celery: 1 heart, not the whole heart but the very center, which
   is the most tender, cut in very small pieces; include the
   leaves
and/or
Onion: ½ small, cut in minute pieces

Combine all the ingredients (have the seafood cool) and refrigerate in an acid resistant bowl for at least 1 hour.
   Remove from the refrigerator ½ hour before serving.

CALAMARI IMBOTTITI

Stuffed Squid

Yield: 4 servings

Squid: 2 pounds; this dish loses a lot if the squid goes through
   even the quickest parboiling, so use only very fresh squid.
   (Read Notes on Cleaning and Preparing Squid, page 50)
Bread crumbs: ¾ cup
Parsley: 2 full sprigs, finely cut; discard the stems
Garlic: 1 clove, cut in minute pieces
Salt: 1 teaspoon
Pepper: freshly ground black, ½ teaspoon
Oil: olive

Make sure the squid hoods are well blotted (including the inside).

Cook the tentacles quickly in a skillet on high heat with some oil; cut into small pieces.

Toast the bread crumbs in a pan with some oil (see recipe for Toasted Bread Crumbs, page 80). As the bread crumbs start taking some color, add the garlic and the onion; keep cooking them until well toasted.

Mix in the parsley, tentacles, salt, and pepper. Divide the stuffing among the hoods—it should fit loosely. (If you have excess stuffing, remove the tentacle pieces, put in the hoods, and sprinkle the remaining stuffing (now mostly bread crumbs) on the hoods before broiling them.

Pin together the opening of the hoods with a toothpick and coat them with oil. Have the broiler pan preheated and as close as allowable to the heat source. Broil the squid 3 to 4 minutes per side, according to size.

Side Dishes
Contorni

During an Italian dinner, vegetables, salads included, are served along with the second course. Side dishes shouldn't be considered secondary or just a way to fill a plate—a carefully chosen and well-matched vegetable can be the key to success of your second course.

The use of vegetable dishes is extended to many parts of the meal. Vegetables cooked with a number of additional ingredients, such as eggplant *parmigiana* with eggs can be considered a substantial enough dish to be the most important part of the second course and can be coupled either with a plain vegetable or with a very simple second course dish. Vegetables can appear as first course or make up the bulk of supper with cheeses, cold cuts, and eggs on the side.

In Sicily raw fennel wedges and radishes, served in a bowl of chilled water, are eaten in place of fruit, with no condiment but a touch of salt. In the spring fresh fava beans and sharp cheese are used to start or finish a meal.

Italians have shared the very bad international habit of overcooking vegetables to the gray point of color and flavor. In Italy vegetables were thought to carry diseases. This was true in the past when the ways of fertilizing fields were unmentionable. But, even though farming practices were modernized several decades ago, the habit of lengthy cooking stayed. Vegetables that suffered the most from it were the ones usually boiled and then stir-fried in oil and garlic or just served with oil. Even as a child I could not understand why anybody would want to eat those string beans and squashes lying flat out on a plate limp and lifeless.

Sensitization to real nutritional values has encouraged shorter cooking times and has improved the quality of many vegetable dishes, both in taste and content. Today no meal is complete without their color, taste, and texture.

INSALATA DI ARANCE ALLA SICILIANA

Sicilian Orange Salad

Yield: 4 to 6 servings

Oranges: 4, navel, peeled; cut in ¼-inch slices widthwise
Oil: olive
Salt: ½ to 1 teaspoon (sour oranges will require more salt)
Pepper: freshly ground black, ½ teaspoon

Mix the sliced oranges with the other ingredients. Arrange in a bowl and let them stand in the refrigerator for about thirty minutes before serving.

The peel, if properly removed, can be used to make Candied Orange Peel (see recipe page 291).

INSALATA DI SPINACI

Spinach Salad

Yield: 4 servings

Spinach: ½ pound, no stems, cut with a very sharp knife into bite-size pieces; roughly ¾-inch strips; large leaves will need to be cut also lengthwise

Lettuce: about ½ pound, Boston, cut in ¾-inch strips

Optional:
Mushrooms: a few, thinly sliced

The cream and garlic salad dressing is particularly good with this combination of vegetables; any of the other dressings will do well. (See Dressing Recipes, page 78.)

Cut your salad shortly before serving, and add the dressing just before serving it.

INSALATA VERDE

Green Salad

Yield: 4 servings

Lettuce: 1 medium-size head, or any of the following vegetables, in combination, or alone: escarole, chicory, or endive. When combining greens for salad, it is best to put together similar leaves, for example mixing romaine with escarole, and Boston lettuce with bib lettuce. Cut the leaves with a very sharp knife, in ¾-inch ribbons; discard the tougher leaves

Optional:

Fennel: 1, small, only the white bulbous part of it and the most
tender feathery leaves. Quartered, cut in thin slices

Use salad dressing or Mustard Dressing; see recipes pages 80
and 81. If you do not add the fennel, you may use also Cream
and Garlic Dressing, page 81.

Cut your salad shortly before serving, and add the dressing
just before serving it.

INSALATA DI POMODORO

Tomato Salad

Yield: 4 to 6 servings

Tomatoes: 4, if large, use comparable number if smaller, ripe,
and firm; cut in half, widthwise, and cut each half in
wedges; remove the stem attachment

Optional: (any or all of the following)

Capers: a few

Olives: a few, black or green

Green leafy vegetables: a few leaves; choose one that isn't
fragile such as romaine or escarole; cut in ¾-inch strips

Watercress: a few sprigs, separated

Fennel: 1, small, cut as in Insalata Verde, page 220

Add the Salad Dressing or Mustard Dressing, pages 80 and 81, a
few minutes before serving.

INSALATA MISTA

Mixed Salad

Yield: 4 to 6 servings

Tomatoes: 2, as in Tomato Salad, page 201

To the tomatoes, add at least 5 of the following ingredients:
Capers: a few, well rinsed if preserved in salt, well drained
Olives: a few, black and/or green
Artichoke: 1, the tenderest part; (see Artichokes: Preparation,
    page 214). Cut in slivers; sprinkle with lemon juice
Celery: 1 to 3 stalks, from the heart, cut in very small pieces
Cucumber: ½, a medium-size one, peeled, quartered, seeds
    removed; cut in ½-inch pieces
Onion: a few spring onions, or ½ small regular onion; cut in
    thin slivers
Eggs: 1 or 2, hard-boiled, in wedges or halves
Anchovies: a few flat fillets, well drained
Tuna: one can, medium or large, packed in water or oil, well
    drained .

Mix the salad and add Salad Dressing or Mustard Dressing,
pages 80 and 81, up to 1 hour before serving.

INSALATA CRUDA E COTTA

Raw and Cooked Salad

Yield: 6 to 8 servings

Tomatoes: 2, as in Tomato Salad, page 201
String beans: ½ pound, parboiled. To parboil beans see Fagio-
    lini Soffritti, page 205
Carrots: 2, medium, cut in very thin rounds
Artichokes: a few slices, preserved in oil
Pickles: some, Italian (preserved in plain vinegar), well drained
Capers: a few; wash well if preserved in salt. Drain well

Optional:
To the above ingredients, you may add any or all of the following:
Asparagus: a few, steamed or parboiled, cut in large sections
Beet: 1 or 2, boiled, sliced
Zucchini: 1, parboiled, cut in ½-inch rounds
Onion: 2, small, baked in the jacket; (see Whole Baked Onions,
    page 210). Remove the peel; cut in large pieces
Potato: 1 or 2, medium, boiled, diced

Add Salad Dressing or Mustard Dressing, pages 80 and 81, to
the cooked vegetables, preferably while they are still hot. Add
the other ingredients except the beets. Add the beets just before
serving the salad.
    The salad should be served while still warm.

SCAROLA SOFFRITTA

Stir-Fried Escarole

Yield: 4 servings

Escarole: about 2 pounds, only the tender leaves; discard the
core the leaves were attached to, leaving the leaves whole.
Steam till tender
Garlic: 2 cloves, slightly crushed in their jackets
Oil: olive
Salt: 1 teaspoon
Pepper: freshly ground black, to taste

Coat the bottom of a wide skillet with a generous layer of oil.
Add the garlic and heat them until aromatic but not burned. If
you wish to remove the garlic, do it at this point.

Add the escarole, stir over very high heat, and add salt and
pepper. Cook, stirring often, for about five minutes. The vegetable should be coated with oil and show no liquid.

Serve hot.

VERDURA CONDITA CON OLIO CRUDO

Greens Dressed with Raw Oil

Yield: 4 servings

Greens: 2 pounds, escarole, chicory, or spinach; only tender
leaves; or, asparagus, zucchini, or yellow squash

Lemon: 2, in wedges
Oil: olive
Salt: to taste
Pepper: freshly ground black, to taste

Steam the greens until tender. Sprinkle on some salt and pepper and arrange on a plate. Trickle some oil on the greens. New oil, fresh from the press, is particularly enjoyable on this very simple dish. Arrange the lemon on the plate. Lemon and oil to be added according to individual taste.

This dish can also be served cold. In Sicily it is often eaten for supper, as a first course.

FAGIOLINI SOFFRITTI

Stir-Fried String Beans

Yield: 4 to 6 servings

String beans: 1½ pounds; cut both ends off. Parboil (bring a good deal of water to a boil, put the beans in, bring back to a boil, and drain as soon as they lose their stiffness but they are still *al dente* and bright green). You may use broccoli— the flowers and the tender part of the stalks. Parboil as the beans
Garlic: 2 cloves
Oil: olive
Salt: 1 teaspoon
Pepper: freshly ground black, ½ teaspoon; or 2 small hot red chilies

Cover the bottom of a wide skillet with a generous coating of oil. Heat the oil with the garlic (and the chilies) until aromatic. Add the beans and cook over high heat, stirring every now and then, for 5 to 10 minutes.

Season with salt and pepper. Remove the garlic (and the chilies) before serving.

FAGIOLINI AL POMODORO

String Beans with Tomato

Yield: 4 to 6 servings

String beans: 1½ pounds, cooked as per Stir-Fried String Beans, see recipe page 205
Tomato sauce: ½ cup, see Tomato Sauce page 88

Add to the string beans the tomato sauce, cover, and cook over medium heat about 10 minutes.

FUNGHI TRIFOLATI

Sautéed Mushrooms

Yield: 4 to 6 servings

Mushrooms: 2 pounds, cut in ⅓-inch slices
Garlic: 4 to 6 cloves, cut in coarse pieces. If you like strong garlic flavor, cut one clove in very small pieces
Parsley: a fistful, cut in very small pieces; discard the stems

Oil: olive
Salt: 1 teaspoon
Pepper: freshly ground black, to taste

Heat a ¼-inch layer of oil in a wide skillet with the coarsely cut garlic. When aromatic, add the mushrooms, stir quickly, and cook over high heat for a few minutes, stirring a couple of times. Turn off heat, add all the other ingredients, and mix well.

ZUCCHINE TRIFOLATE

Sautéed Zucchini

Yield: 6 servings

Zucchini: 8, slender, crisp, preferably dark green; cut off ends, slice in ½-inch rounds
Garlic: 3 cloves, coarsely cut
Oil: olive
Parsley: 4 sprigs, finely cut; discard the stems
Salt: ½ to 1 teaspoon
Pepper: freshly ground black, ½ teaspoon

Cover the bottom of a wide skillet with a generous layer of oil, add the garlic, and heat until aromatic. Add the zucchini, increase to high heat, and cook until they begin to brown, turning them a couple of times.

Cover the pan and let the zucchini cook over low heat until crisp.

Turn off the heat, add the parsley, and season with salt and pepper.

BROCCOLO IN TEGAME

Braised Cauliflower with Anchovies

Yield: 4 servings

Cauliflower: 1, about 2 pounds; cut all the flower tips off, slicing them in ⅓-inch slices. Peel the portion of the stem that is tender, and cut in thin slices
Onion: 1, medium, finely cut in small pieces
Pine nuts: 1 tablespoon
Currants: 1 tablespoon
Salt: ½ teaspoon, or more
Pepper: freshly ground black, ½ teaspoon
Anchovies: 6, flat fillets, preserved in olive oil, mashed
Tomato paste: 1½ teaspoons
Oil: olive, ⅓ to ½ cup

Heat the oil and the onions in a heavy pot until the onions are translucent and aromatic. Add the tomato paste, stirring it in the oil over medium-high heat for a couple of minutes.

Add the cauliflower; stir it over high heat until well coated with the oil and tomato paste. Reduce the heat, add the pine nuts, currants, salt, and pepper; cover and cook over medium-low to low heat for about 30 minutes, or until tender, stirring every now and then. After you turn off the heat, add the anchovies.

This vegetable is used as topping for pasta as well. Pasta topped with it is called *Pasta alla Paolina*.

BROCCOLO AFFOGATO

Braised Cauliflower with Olives

Yield: 4 servings

Cauliflower: 1, about 2 pounds; prepare as Braised Cauliflower
   with Anchovies, page 208
Olives: ¼ pound, black, Sicilian or Greek
Garlic: 2 cloves
Oil: olive, ⅓ to ½ cup
Salt: 1 teaspoon
Pepper: freshly ground black, ½ teaspoon

Heat the oil and the garlic in a heavy pot until aromatic. Add the
cauliflower and cook it over high heat, stirring, for a couple of
minutes.
   Add the olives, salt, and pepper.
   Cover the pot and cook over medium-low to low heat about
30 minutes, stirring every now and then.
   Uncover, increase the heat to high, and cook it, stirring, a few
more minutes until it starts browning and sizzles.

PEPERONI AL PAN GRATTATO

Peppers with Bread Crumbs

Yield: 4 servings

Peppers: 4, very large, fleshy, green or red peppers; remove
   seeds, spongy interior, and stems. Cut in ⅔-inch strips

Bread crumbs: ⅔ cup, plain
Onion: 1, small, cut in very small pieces
Parsley: 2 full sprigs, finely cut, discard the stems
Cheese: 2 tablespoons, grated, *caciocavallo*, or Romano
Pine nuts: 2 teaspoons
Currants: 2 teaspoons
Oil: olive
Salt: to taste
Pepper: freshly ground black, to taste

Cover the bottom of a heavy skillet with olive oil; add the bread crumbs and the onion. Cook stirring over medium heat until the bread crumbs are toasted.

Turn off heat. Add parsley, currants, pine nuts, salt, pepper, and cheese. Heat some oil in a wide skillet and put in the peppers. Cook, stirring over high heat, for a couple of minutes. Then cover and cook over medium-low heat until tender. Remove the cover, increase the heat to high, and stir until all liquid has evaporated. Mix in the bread-crumb mixture. Serve hot or cold.

CIPOLLE INTERE INFORNATE

Whole Baked Onions

Yield: 4 servings

Onions: 12, small, in their jackets; rinse

Place the onions in a low-sided baking dish. Pierce them in a few places. Bake in a preheated oven at 400°F for one hour.

Remove the skin and serve with Salad Dressing, page 80.

CIPOLLETTE CARAMELLATE

Caramelized Pearl Onions

Yield: 4 servings

Pearl onions: 1 pound; to peel the onions, cut off the tips at both ends. Bring a few cups of water to a boil. Dip the onions in, and turn off the heat. Let them stay in the water 1 to 2 minutes. Remove the onions to cold water. Remove the peel and the first coarse layer
Butter: 4 tablespoons, unsalted
Salt: ½ teaspoon
Pepper: freshly ground black, ½ teaspoon
Sugar: 1 tablespoon

Put the onions in a sauce pan with the butter, salt, pepper, sugar, and enough water to cover them halfway.

Bring to a boil, then let them simmer, covered, for 20 minutes, or until tender but not mushy.

Remove them from the liquid and let the liquid boil down to about one third. Add the onions and cook over high heat, stirring, until the liquid coats them in a thick glaze.

Serve them hot or at room temperature.

ZUCCHINE INFORNATE

Baked Zucchini

Yield: 4 servings

Zucchini: 6, skinny, split in one half lengthwise
Oil: olive
Salt: ½ teaspoon
Pepper: freshly ground black, ½ teaspoon

Rub the zucchini halves with salt, pepper, and oil.
   Arrange them in a shallow baking dish, cut side up.
   Bake in preheated oven at 400°F for 20 minutes. Turn them, cut side down, and bake 10 more minutes or until brown.

Variation:

MEZZE CIPOLLE INFORNATE

Baked Onion Halves

Instead of zucchini, or along with them, you may bake onions. The procedure is slightly different.
   Use medium-size onions. Leaving the outermost layer on, cut off the tips and cut the onions in half widthwise. Rub the cut surface with salt, pepper, and oil. (Allow one or two medium-size onions per person.)
   Place them in a low-sided baking pan, peel side down. Add a thin layer of water to the bottom of the pan.
   Bake in oven preheated at 400°F for 40 minutes, or a little longer, basting them every now and then. In the last 10 minutes, turn. When ready they should be brown.

BROCCOLO ALLA SEVERINA

Cauliflower Severina

Yield: 6 to 8 servings

Cauliflower: 3 pounds, weigh after cutting off leaves and hard
    stems. Cook in plenty of boiling water for 5 minutes. Drain
    well. Slice the flower bunches in ½-inch slices
Cheese: ⅓ cup, *caciocavallo* or Romano, grated

Ragú:
Tomato paste: 9 ounce can
Onion: 1 small, cut in minute pieces
Garlic: 2 cloves
Bacon: ¼ pound, cut the slices in three to four pieces
Oil: olive
Salt: 1 teaspoon
Pepper: freshly ground black, ½ teaspoon

Pour enough oil to cover the bottom of a medium-size saucepan. Add the bacon, onion, and garlic; cook until aromatic. Stir
in the tomato paste; add ⅔ cup water, salt, and pepper, mixing
well. Cover and let it cook about 30 minutes.

Grease a baking dish with oil. Layer it with half of the cauliflower, half the sauce, and cover it with the cheese. Layer the
remaining cauliflower over it, and spoon the other half of the
sauce on top.

Bake in oven preheated to 375°F for about thirty minutes.

Stir it well and serve immediately.

Note:
My grandmother Severina's recipe calls for pork skin (*cotenna*);

it is very hard to find, but, if available, use it in place of bacon. Use ½ pound of it, cut in ⅓-inch strips, well scrubbed. Add it to the *Ragú* after the tomato paste and the water. Cook 1½ hours, increase the salt to taste.

Artichokes: Preparation

Given the artichokes we get on the east coast area, it is quite an accomplishment to serve them in any way other than boiled.

In the vegetable world bigger is not always better. Artichokes grow to an ideal size after which any further enlargement is detrimental; as they grow bigger, they also grow tougher. In that case out of a huge artichoke there is a lesser edible part than when the artichoke was half the size.

The cleaning process I suggest for artichokes might sound wasteful, but, in fact, most of what gets discarded is what could never be eaten, even if cooked 24 hours.

Have some lemon halves handy. Cut the stem of the artichoke close to the leaves and pull off a couple of lower leaf layers all around. Start breaking off the leaves, just above where they are attached, and keep breaking off smaller and smaller sections of leaves as you get closer to the core. Breaking them off is better than cutting them off because you can get the feel of where the point is that they start getting too tough, just as you do snapping asparagus. Pressing your thumb down over the lower part of the leaf, bending, and snapping off the other end should break the leaf just at the right spot.

As the artichoke has become about half the size it was, or as the leaves become very light and tender up to their tip, cut off the tip part, about one third down. The leaves left on below the stem will still have a very fibrous outer layer. Peel it off with a very sharp knife, from the stem down.

Quarter the artichoke by digging out the wiry part in the core and cutting off the spiny tips of the smallest leaves inside using a small knife. During the cleaning process rubbing lemon on your fingers and on the artichokes will help keep both from getting stained. If you wish to serve the artichokes whole, don't dig into the core to remove the choke and the spiny interior; it can be very messy. Considering what a treat it is to most people to eat artichokes, they won't mind working on it at the table.

CARCIOFI RIPIENI

Stuffed Artichokes

Yield: 6 servings

Artichokes: 9, cleaned; see previous instructions. Do not quarter them—cut them in half, clean out the choke, and remove the inner leaves' spines. If you have had the luck to find tender, not overgrown artichokes, leave them whole after removing the outer layers of leaves. Cut off top one third of the artichoke

Bread crumbs: 1½ cup, toasted, (see recipe Toasted Bread Crumbs, page 80). If you are using smaller, tender whole artichokes, 1 cup will be enough

Cheese: 3 tablespoons, *caciocavallo* or Romano, grated

Pine nuts: 1 tablespoon

Currants: 1 tablespoon

Onion: 1, very small, finely cut in minute pieces

Parsley: 2 to 3 full sprigs, finely cut; discard the stems

Oil: olive

Salt: ½ teaspoon

Pepper: freshly ground black, ½ teaspoon

Lay the artichoke halves on the bottom of a skillet in one layer (you may need two pans), cut side up. If using whole artichokes, loosen up the leaves by pushing them down on the counter with a rotating motion as you hold them firmly from the stem end. Cut the stems and put them in the pan as well. The artichokes should fit in the pan snugly. Sprinkle salt and pepper on them and trickle on some oil. Add a small amount of water to the bottom of the pan, about ¼-inch layer.

Cover them and let them cook over very low heat until *al dente*. To test for doneness use a skewer, feeling the resistance as you insert it through the leaves. They should be as crisp as you like your other vegetables.

While the artichokes are cooking (steaming), mix the bread crumbs with the onion, cheese, parsley, pine nuts, and currants.

Arrange the artichokes in a low-sided baking dish, leaf ends up, and trickle the pan drippings on them. Distribute the bread crumb mixture on the artichokes, pressing it down, so that it will penetrate some in between the leaves. Bake in preheated oven at 375°F for 10 to 15 minutes. Serve hot or at room temperature.

PIATTO FREDDO DI CARCIOFI E ASPARAGI

Artichoke and Asparagus Cold Plate

Yield: 10 servings

Mayonnaise: see recipe, page 74, use quantity indicated in the recipe

Artichokes: 6, cleaned; see Artichokes: Preparation, page 214. Cut in thick wedges, keep unsliced. Cook as *Zucchine Trifolate*, see recipe, page 207; omit parsley. Chill

Asparagus: 2 pounds, weigh after snapping off the hard end. Steam whole till barely tender; chill

Eggs: 5, hard-boiled. Remove the yolk, and cut the white of 3 in
slices: keep 2 in halves, lengthwise; chill
Tomatoes: a few, very red cherry tomatoes, in thin wedges,
and/or halves; remove all the seeds and the inside fleshy
part
Paprika: ground

Assemble the dish in any way that is pleasing to the eye, using
the slices of egg white and the tomatoes for decoration. Line up
the asparagus with the points toward the edge of the plate.
Arrange the artichokes in between, using the uncut one as the
center. Zigzag the mayonnaise over the vegetables, use the
halved eggs and the yolks to top the plate, and mound on more
mayonnaise. Break the pattern with the tomatoes and egg
whites and sprinkle with paprika.

Refrigerate for a few hours before serving (it will not lose any
flavor if it stays in for 24 hours).

FRITTELLA

Artichokes, Peas, and Fava Beans

Yield: 6 servings

Artichokes: 3, cleaned and cut in ⅓-inch wedges; see Arti-
chokes: Preparation, page 214
Peas: 10 ounces, frozen, or fresh; if fresh, weigh after shelling
Fava beans: 10 ounces, fresh; weigh after shelling. Pick slender
pods—the larger the pod the harder the fava bean. Fava
beans may be replaced by baby lima beans
Onion: 1, medium, cut in very small pieces
Oil: olive

Salt: 1 teaspoon, or to taste
Pepper: freshly ground black, ½ teaspoon

Optional:
Vinegar: ⅓ cup
Sugar: 1 tablespoon

If you are using frozen peas and frozen lima beans, bring a pot full of water to a boil, put the vegetables in, keeping the heat on high, and let them cook until they separate; drain.

If you are using fresh peas and fresh fava beans, assess how tender they are. If the fava beans are large, you should remove the skin (besides the pod) as it can be very tough.

Heat a generous layer of oil and the onion in a 8- to 9-inch pot; when aromatic, add the artichokes. If you have found fresh favas and they are larger than baby lima beans, add them at the same time as the artichokes. Stir the vegetables in the oil, add salt and pepper, cover, and cook over very low heat, stirring occasionally, until *al dente*. Add the peas and the fava beans, or the lima beans. Cover and cook about 10 minutes. Stir a few times.

Frittella can be eaten on pasta; it can be made in advance and reheated or eaten at room temperature. *Frittella* is also served cold, sweet and sour. When the vegetables are done, add the vinegar and the sugar and stir over high heat for a few minutes. Correct the salt; let it cool and serve as an antipasto.

TORTINO DI FINOCCHI

Fennel Baked in Béchamel

Yield: 4 to 6 servings

Fennel: 3, cleaned and quartered, parboiled (cook in plenty of
   boiling water until *al dente*). Cut in ⅓-inch slices, length-
   wise. You may substitute 2 pounds cauliflower for the fen-
   nel, parboiled, sliced as the fennel
Cheese: 6 tablespoons, Parmesan, grated
Cheese: ¼ pound, Jarlsberg or Swiss, in thin slices, or grated
Butter: unsalted
Salt: ½ teaspoon
Pepper: freshly ground black, to taste
Béchamel: 2 cups, see recipe page 73

Preheat oven to 375°F. Butter a baking dish generously—choose
one with low sides. Sprinkle the salt on the fennel and add as
much pepper as you wish.

   Mix the cheeses with the béchamel sauce. Cover the bottom
of the baking dish with fennel and spread a layer of sauce on it.
Add the rest of the fennel and cover with the sauce you have
left.

   Bake 30 minutes or until bubbly.

Eggplants: Preparation

Different recipes suggest various ways of cutting and treating
eggplant before cooking. Whatever the recipe might be tops and
bottoms are always cut off, and the stem end is cut far enough
down to remove any green and fibrous part immediately at-

tached to it. Eggplant can be sliced widthwise in rounds, in which case no peel is removed, or lengthwise.

It is preferable to slice them lengthwise if they are to top pasta or to be used to make little stuffed rolls.

To slice them lengthwise, as the eggplant available in the United States is likely not to be less than 5- or 6-inches long, cut them first in half, widthwise, then slice them (see drawing).

Some recipes call for diced eggplant. To cube the eggplant first cut them across at the point where the eggplant swells out; this makes it easier to control the size of the cubes.

Most of the time, to draw out some of the bitter juices, eggplant is soaked in water and a little salt for thirty minutes, or sprinkled with salt and placed in a colander. A plate is put on top of the eggplant to weigh it down. Pat the slices dry whether soaked in water or just sprinkled with salt; drain the cubes well. Eggplant is seldom peeled, as the skin is a nice addition to the texture that otherwise is very soft.

Note:

If eggplants are not soaked in water, but sprinkled with salt to get rid of the bitter juices, keep them in a colander for 30 minutes or as long as it takes to see some brown liquid draining off them.

MELANZANE FRITTE

Fried Eggplant

Yield: 2 to 4 servings

Eggplant: 1, about 6 inches long, sliced ⅓-inch thick, widthwise or lengthwise, or diced in 1-inch cubes. To cut and prepare eggplant for frying see Eggplants: Preparation, page 219. Soak in water, drain, and pat dry

Oil: olive, enough for eggplant to float in while frying

Fry the eggplant in very hot oil over high heat. If in slices turn and brown the other side when well browned on one side; if in cubes, turn a couple of times until brown all around.

Fried eggplant slices or cubes are a nice addition to pasta with tomato sauce. Cutting the slices lengthwise makes it easier to cut with the fork. With rounds the skin surrounding the slice makes it harder to cut through with the fork.

Also try them stuffed, while still hot, with a little salt sprinkled on top, in a piece of Italian or French bread.

MELANZANE A COTOLETTA

Breaded Eggplants

Yield: 6 servings

Eggplants: 2, 6 to 7 inches long; cut in ⅓-inch rounds, skin on. See Eggplants: Preparation, page 219. Sprinkle with salt, pat dry
Eggs: 2, extra-large, beaten together with a fork
Bread crumbs: About 2 cups, unflavored
Salt: ½ teaspoon or more
Oil: corn or made from seeds

Coat the eggplants first with the egg then with the bread crumbs.

Have enough oil in a heavy skillet to let the eggplant slices float freely. Fry the eggplants over medium-high heat until the crumb coating is golden brown.

Serve hot, sprinkled with salt.

MELANZANE ALLA PARMIGIANA

Eggplant Parmigiana

Yield: 6 to 8 servings

Eggplants: 3, about 6 inches long, cut in slices ⅓-inch thick, fried. To cut and prepare eggplants, see Eggplants: Preparation, page 219, and Fried Eggplant, page 220
Tomato sauce: 3 cups, see *Salsa di Pomodoro*, page 88, use basil as herb
Cheese: 3 ounces, Parmesan, grated
Cheese: ½ pound mozzarella, sliced ¼-inch thick

Arrange all the ingredients in a baking dish, alternating layers of eggplant, mozzarella, tomato sauce, and Parmesan. Repeat until ingredients are used up. End with mozzarella covered with tomato sauce and Parmesan.

Bake in oven preheated to 375°F for 30 to 40 minutes.

MELANZANE ALLA PARMIGIANA ALL'UOVO

Eggplant Parmigiana with Eggs

Yield: 6 to 8 servings

Eggplants: 3, about 6 inches long, cut in slices ⅓-inch thick, fried. To cut and prepare eggplants see Eggplants: Preparation, page 219, and Fried Eggplant, page 220

Tomato sauce: 3 cups, see *Salsa di Pomodoro*, page 88, use basil
    as herb
Cheese: 3 ounces, Parmesan, grated
Cheese: ½ pound mozzarella, sliced ¼-inch thick
Béchamel sauce: 1 cup, see recipe, page 73
Eggs: 2, hard-boiled, sliced in ¼-inch rounds
Ham: ¼ pound, cooked, sliced thin

Arrange all the ingredients in a baking dish, alternating layers of
eggplant, mozzarella, tomato sauce, Parmesan, eggs, ham, and
béchamel. Repeat till you run out of ingredients, ending with
béchamel.
    Bake in oven preheated to 375°F for 45 minutes.

CAPONATA

Caponata, or Sweet and Sour Eggplant

Yield: 10 servings

Eggplants: 4, about 4 pounds, cubed, fried. To cut and prepare
    eggplants, see Eggplants: Preparation, page 219, and Fried
    Eggplant, page 220; save oil
Onion: 1, large, cut in small pieces
Celery: 1 heart, cut in small pieces
Olives: ½ cup, green, pitted, cut in small pieces
Capers: ⅓ cup, preferably preserved in salt, well rinsed
Tomato sauce: 1 cup, see recipe page 88
Vinegar: ⅔ cup, wine
Sugar: 2 tablespoons
Almonds: ½ cup, toasted, crushed; (see Mandorle Brustolite,
    page 79)

In a good-size skillet pour enough of the oil you fried the eggplants in to cover its bottom; add the onion and the celery, cooking until aromatic. Add the tomato sauce, olives, and capers. Increase the heat to high; add vinegar and sugar, stirring for 1 or 2 minutes. Add the fried eggplant and cook over medium heat a couple more minutes. Mix in one half of the almonds. Let it stand a few hours; overnight is better. Serve at room temperature topped with the remaining almonds. Use as a side dish or as an appetizer.

Variation:
To *caponata* you may add cubes of boiled beef, deboned chicken, or boiled octopus cut up in bite-size pieces. Use it as a second course.

MELANZANE ARROSTITE

Roasted Eggplant

Yield: 6 servings

Eggplants: 2, 6- to 7-inches long, cut in ½-inch rounds, skins on; see Eggplants: Preparation, page 219. Sprinkle with some salt. Pat dry
Oil: olive, ⅓ cup
Parsley: 2 full sprigs, cut finely; discard the stems
Garlic: 1 clove, cut in small pieces
Salt: ½ teaspoon
Pepper: freshly ground black, ½ teaspoon

Optional:
Tomatoes: 2, fresh, ripe, peeled, seeded; cut in small pieces
Pepper: ½ a small, red, hot chili, crushed

Place the eggplant slices, patted dry, on a cookie sheet in one layer.

Bake in oven preheated to 450°F for 20 to 30 minutes.

Make a sauce with the oil, parsley, garlic, salt, and pepper. If you wish, add the tomatoes and chili.

Remove the slices from the cookie sheet with a spatula. (Eggplant slices may be difficult to handle, as they may stick to the cookie sheet.) Put them in a bowl in layers, spooning some sauce on each. Eat hot or at room temperature.

MELANZANE A "CANAZZO"

Eggplant and Assorted Vegetables

Yield: 6 servings

Eggplants: 1, 6- to 7-inches, cut in cubes, about 1 inch around, soaked in water and salt, well drained; see Eggplants: Preparation, page 219
Potatoes: 2, small, peeled, diced in ¾-inch pieces
Pepper: 2; clean out the spongy interior and the seeds. Cut in 1-inch squares
Tomatoes: 2, large, fresh, very ripe, but firm and fleshy; or 4, good-size, canned, peeled. Seed and cut in small pieces
Onion: 1, small, cut in small pieces
Oil: olive
Salt: 1½ teaspoons
Pepper: freshly ground black, ½ teaspoon

Pour a good layer of oil in a large pot, add the onions, and cook until aromatic. Add the eggplant, potatoes, and peppers, stirring them around over medium-high heat until well coated with oil. Add the tomatoes, season with salt and pepper, cover, and let them cook over low heat stirring every now and then until done about 30 to 45 minutes. If the tomatoes have released a lot of liquid, evaporate it by stirring the vegetables uncovered over medium-high heat.

Note:

In Sicilian dialect *canazzo* is a derogatory term for dog.

MELANZANE AL POMODORO

Eggplant in Tomato Sauce

Yield: 6 to 8 servings

Eggplants: 3, about 6- to 7-inches long, peeled, diced in 1-inch pieces, deep fried until lightly browned. In this recipe eggplants are not put through soaking or salt sprinkling

Tomato sauce: 2 cups, see recipe page 88

Basil: a few leaves; if only dry basil is available, ½ teaspoon. Or, instead of basil, use mint

Salt: to taste

Pepper: to taste, freshly ground black

Add the eggplants to the tomato sauce, bring to a boil, simmer covered for 15 minutes. Add the basil and salt and pepper, if necessary, after tasting. As the eggplants haven't released their bitter juices before cooking, the dish will have some bite to it, and the addition of seasoning is up to the individual taste.

May be served on pasta.

Note:

To fry the eggplant cubes use plenty of olive oil. See recipe, Fried Eggplant, page 220.

PATATE FRITTE

Fried Potatoes

Yield: 4 servings

Potatoes: 2½ pounds, peeled, cut in chunks, about 1½- to 2-inches around
Oil: olive
Salt: to taste

Pour a layer of oil, a little over ½-inch high, in a frying pan; heat well. Add the potatoes, turn the heat to low, and let them cook for 30 to 40 minutes. Turn once after about 20 minutes.

Place them on a paper towel to blot the excess oil; sprinkle with salt.

Serve hot.

PATATE AL FORNO

Baked Potatoes

Yield: 6 servings

Potatoes: 4 pounds, peeled, cut in chunks, about 1½- to 2-inches around
Oil: olive, 6 tablespoons
Rosemary: 1 teaspoon
Salt: ½ teaspoon
Pepper: freshly ground black, ½ teaspoon

Put the oil, rosemary, salt, and pepper in a low-sided baking dish. Add the potatoes and coat them with the seasoned oil.

Bake in oven preheated to 400°F for 1 hour and 10 minutes, or more, until the potatoes have a crisp-golden coating. Halfway through baking, baste the potatoes with the oil.

Serve immediately.

PATATE A SPEZZATINO

Potato Stew

Yield: 6 servings

Potatoes: 6, large, peeled, diced
Onion: 1, medium, cut in small pieces
Oil: olive
Parsley: 3 to 4 sprigs, finely cut; discard the stems
Water: some
Salt: to taste
Pepper: freshly ground black, to taste

Cover the bottom of a pan with a good layer of oil. Add the onion and cook until aromatic. Then add potatoes and stir until well-coated with oil. Add some water (about ½ cup), one half of the parsley, salt, and pepper.

Cover and cook over low heat, stirring frequently, until done about 30 to 45 minutes. To speed the cooking you may add more water and increase heat to medium, stirring frequently to prevent scorching.

When done, after turning off heat, add remaining parsley and correct seasoning.

PATATE A SFINCIONE

Sicilian Potato Pizza

Yield: 6 servings

Potatoes: 2 pounds, baking or Russet, peeled; slice in rounds ⅛-inch thick. Soak in cold water and ½ teaspoon salt for 5 minutes. Drain well
Tomatoes: 2 generous cups, peeled, seeded; cut in small pieces. Keep the juice collected while cleaning out the seeds
Onion: ¾ pound, in very thin slices
Cheese: ½ pound *caciocavallo* (or use the Italian sharp cheese locally made, see *Panzerotti*, page 72, or some sharp provolone) in slices ⅛-inch thick
Cheese: 2 to 3 ounces Romano, grated
Oil: olive, ¼ cup
Salt: ¾ teaspoon
Pepper: freshly ground black, 1 teaspoon
Oregano: 2 teaspoons

Grease a baking dish well with some oil. Choose one where you'll be able to fit the potatoes in three layers, alternating with the other ingredients, and where the final layer will be over ½ inch below the edge of the dish.

Mix the tomatoes with the juice collected while seeding them; add the grated cheese, salt, pepper, oregano, and the oil. Place one layer of potatoes in the baking pan then add about one third of the tomato mixture. Spread over it a layer of onions and add one layer of sliced cheese. Repeat until you run out of ingredients, ending with cheese moistened with tomato mixture.

Bake in a preheated oven at 375°F about 1½ hours.

PATATE ALLA GHIOTTA

Glutton's Potatoes

Yield: 4 to 6 servings

Potatoes: 6, large, baking or regular, in small dices
Oil: olive, ⅓ to ½ cup
Onion: 1, medium, finely cut in small pieces
Garlic: 3 cloves, finely cut in small bits
Tomatoes: 5 to 6, large, peeled, or fresh and ripe, seeded, cut in small pieces
Basil: a few leaves, fresh, or 1 teaspoon, dry
Salt: 1½ teaspoons
Pepper: freshly ground black, 1 teaspoon
Cheese: ½ pound sharp, Italian, in small dices, see *Panzerotti* recipe, page 72

Optional:
Reduce potato quantity to add:
Zucchini: 2, cubed
Eggplant: 1, very small, cubed, soaked in water and salt, well drained; see Eggplants: Preparation, page 219

Heat oil and cook onion until translucent; add garlic, tomatoes, salt, pepper, and basil.

Add potatoes and enough water to barely cover them. Cover and cook over low heat until done. If you chose to add zucchini and eggplant, put them in when potatoes are halfway done. While still hot, top with cheese, cover, and keep in a warm place for 5 to 10 minutes before serving. Serve, preferably in same pot that *ghiotta* has been cooked.

Remember to stir a few times while cooking, to prevent scorching and uneven heating.

Desserts

Piatti di Fine Pasto: Frutta e Dolci

In Italy the way to end an everyday dinner or supper is with fruit. Sweets also appear quite often, along with the fruit, to mark holidays and special occasions. As a rule, sweets are not prepared in the homes. Every neighborhood in an Italian town has its bars and *i caffè* that, besides serving espresso and drinks, are stocked up with a variety of pastries. Back from Sunday morning rides, games, meetings with friends, or church, people crowd their favorite bar to get a fresh supply of sweets for one o'clock dinner.

The dessert mode and taste changes from town to town and from bar to bar. I am very partial to some bars in Palermo where you can find the widest range of pastry, from the lightest to the richest from the airiest to the heaviest and along with it, the delight of summer days, ice cream cakes.

Father loved the sweets, and so did I. On Sunday mornings, we first visited my grandparents, took the dog to run in the park, and then made the ritual stop at the Pasticceria Svizzera or at Caflisch or at some equally good source of pastries. Even in the winter we often walked to get there rather than drive as that season is very mild. It was a pleasure to stroll along Viale Libertá. Keeping my nose up, I would try to catch a glimpse of green in the branches of the sycamores lining the boulevard and enjoy the warmth of the sun while the air had just a touch of chill to it.

I was not an indiscriminate sweet eater; I had high standards and would not touch anything with sugary frostings or glazes. I could do without fruit pies and custard fillings, and I never considered ricotta-filled pastry, because that mother could make so well.

Confronted by chestnut desserts, mounds of beignets, crunchy meringues, puff pastry filled with cream and fresh fruit, and thick chocolate rolls called *Africani*, among other delights, I had a terrible time making up my mind as to what I wanted. I hopped from one end of the display case to the other while the server on the other side held up a cardboard tray, tapping nervously on it with a pair of tongs.

We finally made it out of there, the tray full, and rushed home, where the sound of the key in the lock was enough for mother to start cooking pasta.

In Sicilian cooking, sweets more than any other dish, are an artful construction, a display of color, a combination of tradition and individualism. Some of the pastry I particularly miss I have recreated from memory. I recall how it looked, crunched, or melted when eaten. Things that seemed lost in time and impossible to capture have appeared out of my hands, and I have felt there has been a little magic to it. I hope now that I can give it to others.

WAYS TO SERVE FRESH FRUIT

Strawberries: Sprinkle with white wine vinegar or apple vinegar and a touch of sugar

Apples: Peel, core, slice; sprinkle with lemon juice and some sugar

Peaches: Peel, core, slice; cover with dry white wine

Mixed Fruit: Peel (peel even grapes), slice; add whole blanched almonds, cut in small pieces; mix with vodka or light rum; top with sweetened whipped cream

ARANCE ALLA VODKA

Oranges in Vodka

Oranges: 1 per person, navel, peeled, cut in ⅓-inch slices
   widthwise, seeded. The peel, if properly removed, can be
   used to make Candied Orange Peel; see recipe, page 291
Vodka: 1 tablespoon per orange
Sugar: 1 teaspoon per orange, or to taste

Arrange the slices in layers in a serving dish, sprinkling vodka
and sugar in between the layers. Chill; it is best if served one or
two hours after prepared.

   You may serve them topped with orange or other sherbet.

PERE COL FORMAGGIO

Pears and Cheese

Pears: 1 to 2 per person, ripe at room temperature
Cheese: at least 2 of the following: *mascarpone,* Fontina, Bel
   Paese, *robbiola,* Gorgonzola, provolone, at room temperature

Serve the pears and cheeses on separate plates. Cheese and
pears are supposed to be eaten together. Pears are supposed to
be peeled by each person before eating.

PERE INFORNATE

Baked Pears

Yield: 6 to 8 servings

Pears: 6, ripe, peeled, cored, and cut in half lengthwise
Sugar: 3 tablespoons
Water: some
Cream: 1½ cup, heavy. Whip until very stiff; see Cream, page 41
Chocolate: ¼ ounce, semisweet, shaved into slivers with a sharp knife
Cinnamon: ground

Preheat the oven to 400°F. Place the pear halves close together, cut side up, in a shallow baking pan. Sprinkle with sugar and some water. Pour some more water in the pan to barely cover the bottom.

Bake 1 hour, or until done, but not mushy. While baking, check a few times, and keep adding water as it evaporates. Baste the pears once or twice with juices. Remove from the oven. Turn the pears flat side down; let them cool. Arrange in a serving plate flat side up; chill. If the syrup from the baking is too caramelized thin with a little water stirring over very low heat.

Arrange the cream on pear halves, shaping it in mounds. Sprinkle cinnamon and chocolate on top, then trickle the syrup over the cream mounds. You may serve them immediately or up to a couple of hours after adding the cream.

If you wish to prepare them in advance, you may keep the baked pears refrigerated for several days; keep the pan juices as well. When ready to serve, add the other ingredients.

GELO DI MELONE

Watermelon Pudding

Yield: 4 servings

Watermelon: 3 cups, juice. To obtain the juice, squeeze and
    mush the watermelon through a cheesecloth-lined colander
Cornstarch: 3 tablespoons
Sugar: ¼ cup, or more, depending on the sweetness of the
    watermelon
Chocolate: ½ ounce, semisweet, in small bits
Citron: 1 tablespoon, cut very small
Pistachio: 1 tablespoon, raw, unsalted, shelled, coarsely
    crushed
Jasmine flowers: a few

In a saucepan, mix the cornstarch and the sugar well. Add the
watermelon juice in very small quantities, stirring until you
obtain a thin paste. Add the rest of the juice.

Cook, stirring constantly in one direction, over medium heat
until thick. Pour into a serving dish or individual dishes while
still warm. Let it cool.

Mix the chocolate, the citron, and the pistachio; sprinkle it on
top of the pudding. Insert some jasmine flowers in the pudding
so that the petals rest on the surface. Serve cold.
Note:
Jasmine flowers are hard to find. They are a nice addition but
not indispensable.

CREMA AL CIOCCOLATO

Chocolate Pudding

Yield: 4 servings

Milk: 2 cups
Cocoa: 2 tablespoons, unsweetened
Cornstarch: 2½ tablespoons
Sugar: ¼ cup

Optional:
Chocolate: ½ ounce, semisweet, cut in small bits
Walnuts: ¼ to ½ cup, toasted, crushed; see Oven Roasted
    Nuts, page 67
Cocoa powder: some

Mix the cocoa, cornstarch, and sugar together in a small saucepan.

Slowly add ¼ cup milk, stirring well, to form a smooth paste. Thin it by stirring in little by little some more milk.

Add the rest of the milk.

Cook, stirring, over medium heat. Always stir in one direction, with an even and quick circular motion, down to the bottom of the pan from the center toward the sides and back to the center. The mixture will start thickening as it approaches the boiling point. Reduce to low heat, keep stirring, and cook a couple of minutes more. If you are not adding the chocolate and the walnuts, pour the pudding while still hot in a serving bowl or into individual serving dishes.

If you want to add the chocolate and walnuts, let the pudding cool. Remove and discard the skin formed on top, fold chocolate and walnuts in gently, and spoon into serving dish or dishes.

Instead of folding in the chocolate and the walnuts, you may top the pudding with whipped cream, and sprinkle on it the walnuts, chocolate, and cocoa powder.

Serve well chilled.

CREMA AL CIOCCOLATO CHANTILLY

Chocolate Pudding Chantilly

Yield: 6 to 8 servings

Chocolate pudding: 2 cups; see recipe page 236

Cream: 1 cup, heavy, whipped till very stiff; see notes on Cream, page 41

Sugar: 1 to 2 tablespoons; add to the cream while it is being whipped when it reaches a light stage

Have the pudding cool. Remove and discard the skin formed on top. Fold the cream in gently, start with about one third, working it in until well blended. Then add the rest. You might want to keep some cream to add as decoration.

Spoon into a serving bowl or in individual dishes. Serve chilled, topped with shavings of chocolate, or toasted walnuts, crushed. (See Oven Roasted Nuts, page 67.)

CREMA AL CAFFE

Coffee Pudding

Yield: 4 servings

Milk: 1½ cups
Coffee: ½ cup, very strong Italian espresso. To make the coffee
follow instructions on Espresso Making, page 296
Sugar: ¼ cup
Cornstarch: 2½ tablespoons

Stir coffee and milk together. Mix the sugar and the cornstarch
in a small saucepan. Add the liquid to the dry ingredients as in
Chocolate Pudding, recipe page 236, and follow the same cooking procedure described in that recipe.

Spoon into a bowl or into individual serving dishes. Serve
cold.

You might want to top it with toasted hazelnuts, crushed; see
recipe Oven Roasted Nuts, page 67. Or you might want to pour
some coffee liqueur on top just before serving, or spoon
mounds of whipped cream on top, centered by a coffee bean or a
whole toasted hazelnut.

CREMA AL CAFFE CHANTILLY

Coffee Pudding Chantilly

Yield: 6 to 8 servings

Coffee pudding: 2 cups; (see recipe page 238)
Cream: 1 cup, heavy, whipped till very stiff. (See notes on
    Cream, page 41)
Sugar: 1 to 2 tablespoons; add to the cream as it is being whip-
    ped when it reaches the light stage

Have the pudding cool. Remove and discard the skin formed on
top. Fold the cream in gently, starting with about one third, and
work it in until well blended. Then add and fold in the rest. You
might want to keep some cream to add as decoration.

Spoon into a serving bowl or in individual dishes. You may
serve it topped with light shavings of chocolate, a sprinkle of
cocoa powder, or finely ground toasted hazelnuts. (See Oven
Roasted Nuts, page 67.)

CREMA GIALLA

Milk and Egg Pudding

Yield: 4 servings

Milk: 2 cups
Cornstarch: 2 tablespoons
Sugar: ¼ cup

Egg yolks: 3, remove the white attachments clinging to them, break them with a fork, and mix them together till fairly homogeneous

In a small saucepan mix cornstarch and sugar together well. Add a small amount of milk and stir it in until you obtain a smooth paste. Add more milk to thin it out.

Add some milk to the egg yolks, stirring until well blended. Mix in the rest of the milk and pour it, stirring, in the pan with the cornstarch mixture.

Place it over medium heat. Stir constantly, in one direction, well down to the bottom, all around the edges to the center of the pan. The mixture will start to thicken near the boiling point; stir a couple of minutes past the boiling point. Remove from the heat. Place in a serving bowl or in individual small dishes.

Serve it cold, plain or topped with whipped cream, fresh fruit, slivers of chocolate, or orange or apricot preserve. Accompany with plain cookies.

CREMA GIALLA CHANTILLY

Milk and Egg Pudding Chantilly

Yield: 4 to 8 servings

Milk and egg pudding: 2 cups, as per recipe page 239
Cream: 1 cup, heavy, whipped until very stiff (see notes on Cream, page 41)
Sugar: 2 tablespoons; add to the cream as it is being whipped when it reaches the light stage

Have the pudding cool. Remove the skin formed on top. Fold the cream in gently, starting with about one third, and work it in until well blended. Then add the rest. You might want to keep some cream to add as decoration.

Spoon into a serving bowl or into individual dishes. Serve it as the Milk and Egg Pudding, see page 239.

BIANCO MANGIARE

White Pudding

Yield: 4 servings

Milk: 2 cups

Marzipan: 4 ounces; use the prepared marzipan or almond paste available in stores. Cut in small pieces, or use 3 ounces blanched almonds, ground into a paste

Cornstarch: 3 tablespoons

Sugar: 2 tablespoons, if you use store-bought marzipan, that contains sweeteners. If you use almonds, increase sugar to ¼ cup

Mix cornstarch and sugar in a small saucepan; add a little milk to it. Stir to form a smooth paste. Thin it out with a little more milk.

Place the marzipan or the almond paste in a small saucepan, add about ¼ cup of milk, and stir over low heat until there are no lumps. Stir in the remaining milk and add it to the cornstarch paste.

Cook as the Chocolate Pudding; see recipe page 236

Pour into a serving dish or into individual dishes while still hot.

You may top it with slivers of toasted almonds; see Oven

Roasted Nuts, page 67, or you may top with thin shavings of chocolate or Amaretto liqueur.

Serve with light cookies, such as wafers, if you wish.

RISO COL LATTE

Rice Pudding

Yield: 6 to 8 servings

Rice: ¾ cup best quality Japanese rice or Italian rice for risotti
Milk: 4 cups
Sugar: ½ cup
Vanilla: ½ teaspoon

Stir together the rice, milk, and sugar in a saucepan. Bring it to a boil, uncovered, over medium heat; stir occasionally. Adjust the heat so that the pudding will simmer, uncovered. Let it cook for twenty minutes, then add the vanilla, toward the end of cooking. While the pudding is cooking, watch it closely. Stir it often and make sure that while it stays at a low boil the bottom doesn't get scorched.

While still hot pour it in a low-sided serving dish. I think the delicate taste of this pudding is best appreciated eaten plain. If you want to present it with a more interesting appearance, decorate the edges and the top with a row of slivered almonds.

CREMA DI RICOTTA

Ricotta Cream

Yield: About 2 cups

Ricotta: 1 pound; (read Notes on Ricotta, page 42). To drain
   excess liquid (if there is any) line a colander with cheesecloth, put ricotta in it, and shake it up and down a few times.
   Keep in the colander and put in the refrigerator to give the
   excess liquid time to drain
Sugar: 7 to 10 tablespoons
Citron: 1 tablespoon, candied, finely minced. May use candied
   papaya instead
Chocolate: ½ ounce, semisweet, cut in very small bits

Beat ricotta and sugar with a mixer until smooth; stir in chocolate and citron. Filling will keep for a few days, refrigerated,
without losing any quality. Use as called for by some of the
following dessert recipes.

CREMA MOKA

Mocha Buttercream

Yield: enough to spread on and between a 2- to 3-layer, 10-inch
cake

Butter: ¾ pound, unsalted at room temperature
Sugar: ½ cup, granulated
Coffee: ¾ cup very strong Italian espresso, see Espresso Mak-
   ing, page 296

Optional:
Cocoa powder: 1 or 2 teaspoons

Add the sugar to the coffee and stir it over very low heat until dissolved. Do not let the coffee come to a boil. Let it cool. Beat the butter with an electric mixer at medium to high speed (use speed 6 for the Kitchen Aid) until creamy and light. Add, while still beating, the sweetened coffee in small quantities. Scrape bowl and beater often. The cream will have a light color and texture and a definite coffee flavor.

If you wish to add the cocoa powder, do so just before you start adding the coffee.

Refrigerate it until it reaches a spreading consistency. This can be made in advance and kept in the refrigerator for a few days. Let it soften for a while before spreading.

Use to fill and top pastry and cakes. Use sparingly, as it is very rich. For decoration use whole coffee beans, toasted walnuts, hazelnuts (Oven Roasted Nuts, page 67), chocolate shavings, cocoa powder, or whipped cream.

CREMA AL BURRO E CIOCCOLATO

Chocolate Buttercream

Yield: enough to spread on and between a 2 to 3 layer, 10-inch, cake

Butter: ¾ pound, unsalted at room temperature
Chocolate: 4 ounces, semisweet, melted in a double boiler (see Chocolate Covered Candied Orange Peel, page 292). Cool
Amaretto: 2 ounces. You may use a similar liqueur, like Frangelico, made from hazelnuts, or *nocino*, made from walnuts

Beat the butter with an electric beater at medium-high speed (speed 6 for the Kitchen Aid) until light, about 4 to 5 minutes. Add the melted chocolate; blend it well. Add the liqueur and beat well.

Refrigerate until stiff enough to spread. This can be made days in advance and refrigerated; but allow it to soften before using.

See Mocha Buttercream, page 243, and use similarly.

MOUSSE AL CAFFE

Coffee Mousse

Yield: 10 servings

Egg whites: 4 at room temperature
Cream: 1⅓ cup, heavy, very cold; read the notes on Cream, page 41. Whip in a chilled bowl
Coffee: 1½ cup Italian coffee, very strong; see Espresso Making, page 296. Have 1 cup room temperature, ½ cup cold
Rum: ⅓ cup
Sugar: ½ cup
Vanilla: ½ teaspoon
Cream of tartar: ¼ teaspoon
Gelatin: 2 envelopes, unflavored

Optional:
Walnuts: ½ cup, toasted 5 minutes in 375°F oven, crushed
Chocolate: ½ square, semisweet chocolate, in shavings

Sprinkle gelatin over the 1 cup of coffee at room temperature; dissolve, stirring, over low heat. Cool. Beat the egg whites until foamy; add the cream of tartar, and beat, adding sugar by the spoonful until stiff. Place bowl with cream in a pan containing several inches of ice and water. Add to coffee-gelatin mixture the ½ cup cold coffee, rum, and vanilla, stirring well. Fold one half of the coffee mixture into the egg whites; fold this into the whipped cream. Fold remaining coffee-gelatin mixture into cream-egg-white mixture. Refrigerate. After 4 to 5 minutes, fold over the contents of the bowl with a spatula.

Check, at 5-minute intervals, 2 or 3 more times. Fold over if not blended. You have to keep checking and folding the mousse to make sure that it doesn't set in two layers; a gelatinous bottom and a light creamy top. If that happens, in spite of your close surveillance, do not despair! Instead of sprinkling the walnuts and the chocolate on top, cut them into the mousse; they will give it an interesting texture. As soon as the mousse is blended and almost set (that could be as soon as you check the second time), spoon it into individual dishes or in a large serving bowl, well chilled.

If you choose to use the chocolate, and/or the walnuts, sprinkle them on top before serving.

MOUSSE DI FRAGOLE

Strawberry Mousse

Yield: 8 servings

Strawberries: about 4 cups. Fill 2 cups using only the red outer layer of the strawberries, discard the white, spongy interior. Keep the remaining strawberries whole. Puree enough of the outer layer to fill one cup. Use a food processor, preferably the plastic blade. (I think that strawberry taste is af-

fected by metal.) Cut in small pieces what is left of the red
layer
Jam: ½ cup, strawberry
Cream: 1 cup, heavy
Water: ⅓ cup
Gelatin: 1 envelope, unflavored
Sugar: 3 tablespoons

Blend the pureed strawberries with the jam.

Sprinkle the gelatin on the water and dissolve it over medium-low heat. Add it to the strawberry mixture; blend well. Place it in the refrigerator for five minutes. In the meantime, whip the cream until very stiff (read Cream, page 41). Add the 3 tablespoons of sugar to the cream at the light, fluffy stage. Place the bowl with the cream in a pan containing several inches of ice and water. Fold about one third of the cream in the strawberry-gelatin mixture, then fold the mixture in the cream.

Refrigerate and follow the same checking and folding procedure described in the Coffee Mousse, see recipe page 245.

When it sets, fold in the remaining pieces of the strawberries. Spoon into a bowl or into individual dishes and decorate the mousse with the whole strawberries just before serving.

CREMA CARAMELLA

Baked Custard

Yield: 4 servings

Milk: 2 cups; or substitute ½ cup milk with ½ cup heavy cream
Eggs: 1, extra-large, whole; 3 egg yolks. If you wish to unmold the custard, add 1 egg white

Salt: a pinch
Vanilla: ½ teaspoon
Sugar: ¼ cup

Optional:
Lemon rind: ¼ teaspoon

Caramel coating:
Sugar: ⅔ cup
Water: 4 tablespoons

Beat milk, eggs, vanilla, sugar, salt, and lemon rind until well blended. If you are substituting some milk with cream, stir the cream in last. Have ready a warm oven-proof dish, or 4 individual oven-proof custard dishes; warming the dish will prevent the caramel from freezing when you'll pour it in.

In a small heavy saucepan slowly stir ⅔ cup sugar and the water over medium-low heat until sugar turns a golden honey-like color. Pour into baking dish(es).

Turn dish around quickly to make sure caramel is evenly distributed on the sides and the bottom. Pour in the milk mixture.

Place a rack in a low-sided baking dish, wide enough to accommodate custard dish(es). Pour some hot water up to the rack. Place the custard-filled dish(es) on the rack.

Bake in preheated oven at 300°F for 1¼ hour or longer. When ready it should look like set gelatin. Serve cold.

If you wish to unmold the custard, wait until it is thoroughly cold. If, once unmolded, it pulls apart, you can spread a layer of whipped cream on the cracked top; it will save the look of your dessert and make it richer!

TORTA SEMPLICE

Yellow cake

Yield: enough for 4 layers, about 10 inches in diameter

Flour: 2 cups, unbleached, all-purpose
Eggs: 4, extra-large, whole, plus 2 whites at room temperature
Milk: ⅔ cup
Sugar: 1 cup
Baking powder: 3 teaspoons, double acting
Shortening: ½ cup, margarine or butter, unsalted, melted
Vanilla: 1 teaspoon
Salt: 1 teaspoon

Grease and dust with flour two 10-inch round cake pans.

Mix the flour, salt, and baking powder. Beat the egg yolks and the sugar with an electric beater at medium speed until light—about 5 minutes. Add the shortening and beat until well blended. Start adding the milk and the flour mixture alternately, by quarters. Reduce the speed to low when you first add them then increase it back to medium as they begin getting mixed in. Beat well after each addition and scrape the bowl and the beaters occasionally. Add the vanilla with the last addition of milk.

Beat the egg whites until stiff. Fold immediately in the batter. Bake in oven preheated at 350°F for about 30 minutes. The cake is done when the sides pull from the pan edges and the top has a nice golden color.

Suggestion for filling:
Sprinkle on the layers light rum or vodka mixed with a couple of

tablespoons of orange juice and fill them with Milk and Egg Pudding, page 239; or Chocolate Pudding, page 236; or Ricotta Cream, page 243; or sweetened whipped cream, page 41) and berries.

For the topping, use the filling and/or whipped cream. Decorate the cake filled with chocolate or ricotta with chocolate shavings; for the cake filled with milk and egg pudding, or with cream and berries, decorate with cream and berries.

ZUPPA INGLESE

Zuppa Inglese

Yield: 10 servings

Yellow cake: about ½ pound, in thin slices, enough for two or three layers (see recipe page 249)
Milk and egg pudding: about 4 cups, see recipe page 239. You may use the Chantilly instead of the plain one (see recipe page 240)
Peaches: 8 halves, canned in syrup, in thin slices
Rum: 4 to 6 tablespoons, light

Optional:
Banana: 1, in very thin slices

Assemble and serve your *zuppa inglese* in a glass or crystal bowl. Arrange on the bottom a layer of cake sprinkled with rum and cover it with pudding and fruit slices. (You might want to place some fruit slices against the sides of the bowl so that they will show through.) Keep adding layers in the same order, ending with pudding; decorate with fruit slices.

Serve cold.

TORTA ALLA MANDORLA

Almond Cake

Yield: enough for 4 layers, about 10 inches in diameter

Same ingredients as Torta Semplice, page 249
except:
Sugar: use only ½ cup
And *add* to the ingredients:
Marzipan: 8 ounces, the prepared mix available in stores; cut it
   in small pieces

Warm up ½ cup milk with the marzipan, do not let it boil. Beat until smooth, then beat in the remaining milk.
To mix and bake the cake, follow the same instructions as for Yellow Cake, page 249, using the milk-marzipan mixture for the plain milk.

Suggestion for filling:
Sprinkle on the layers light rum or vodka, mixed, if you wish, with a couple of tablespoons of orange juice, and fill with Chocolate Buttercream, page 244; or Chocolate Pudding, page 236; or White Pudding, page 241. Use the same for the top layer; or use chocolate coating as per Chocolate Covered Candied Orange Peel, page 292.

Or sprinkle on the layers Amaretto or another nut liqueur, and fill with Mocha Buttercream, page 243, or Almond Filling, page 275.

For the top layer of the mocha-filled cake, use the same filling, or chocolate coating; for the cake filled with Almond Filling use Apricot Glaze, page 252.

Decorate the top of the cake with extra filling, toasted hazelnuts or walnuts (Oven Roasted Nuts, page 67), or shavings of chocolate. Sprinkle the top with cocoa powder if you wish.

GHIACCIA

Glaze

Jam: ½ cup, apricot or orange; or use preserves
Water: ½ cup, cold

Mix preserve and water well in a small saucepan. Cook over medium-high heat, stirring; reduce heat if it dries out too fast; start testing after about five minutes. Drop some liquid on a cool surface; touch it—if it is very sticky the glaze is ready. Repeat testing every minute until it reaches the right consistency.

The consistency of the glaze, and the color, when ready, will be very close to that of warmed up honey.

Use the glaze while hot.

Note:

You may make your glaze using your favorite jam.

TIMBALLO ALL' ITALIANA

Italian Timbale

Yield: 9-inch timbale

Potatoes: 18 ounces, white, boiled in the jackets, peeled, pureed; cool off potatoes before pureeing
Almonds: 1 cup, blanched, finely ground
Eggs: 6, extra-large, room temperature; separate yolks from whites
Sugar: 9 tablespoons

Lemon: one-half, peel in very small pieces; *or* may use orange
   peel
Chocolate: ½ ounce, semisweet, in thin shavings
Butter: some, unsalted; or margarine
Bread crumbs: some, unflavored
Cream: 1 cup, heavy

Optional:
Amaretto: a few drops

Beat the potato puree, yolks, and 7 tablespoons sugar with an electric beater on medium speed about 2 minutes. Mix in the almonds and the lemon peel.

Grease well with butter or margarine a high-sided baking dish, about 9 inches in diameter. Dust it with plenty of bread crumbs. Beat egg whites until very airy but not dry.

Fold in the potato mixture about one quarter of the egg white. When well blended, fold in the remaining egg white. Pour in the crumb coated pan and bake in a preheated oven at 350°F for 45 minutes.

Let it cool and unmold it. Refrigerate.

Timbale may be moistened with amaretto. Cover timbale with cream and chocolate shavings. Beat cream. When it is whipped to a light stage add 2 tablespoons of sugar; keep beating until very stiff (see Cream, page 41).

PANETTONE

Italian Christmas Cake

Yield: a very large loaf

Flour: 5 cups, unbleached, all-purpose
Egg yolks: 12, from extra-large eggs
Butter: ½ pound, unsalted
Sugar: 1 cup
Yeast: 2 tablespoons
Salt: 2 teaspoons
Vanilla: 3 teaspoons
Milk: ½ cup, warm
Water: ½ cup, warm
Raisins: 2 cups, dark, seedless
Candied fruit: 1 cup, mixed: use citron, orange peel, honey
    dipped papaya, cut in very small pieces
Rum: ½ cup, light

Dissolve in the water 1 tablespoon of sugar. Add the yeast and dissolve it. Knead it with 1 cup flour. Place it in a bowl, and let it rise until double in bulk.

In the meantime soak the raisins and the candied fruit in the rum. Beat the egg yolks with the remaining sugar until light, about five minutes. (I have used my counter-top Kitchen Aid mixer with the wire beater.) Add the butter and beat until fairly smooth. Mix the salt with two cups of the flour, add it to the yolk mixture, and beat until smooth. Drain the fruit and toss it with ½ cup flour. Switch to a flat beater. Add to the yolk mixture the raised yeast dough; beat until well blended. Add the vanilla to the milk and start adding the milk alternately to the remaining flour in quarters. Beat very well after each addition, and scrape the bowl and the beater a couple of times.

After you have beaten in the last of the flour and the milk, the dough should string from the beater to the bowl sides. Let the dough rise to double its size.

In the meantime prepare your baking dish. You need a round pan about 9 inches in diameter and 5 inches high. Grease it. Line the bottom and the sides with wax paper and grease that as well. If your pan is a little lower than 5 inches, you can double the wax paper lining along the sides and have it come up in a collar. After the dough has risen, beat it down and mix in the fruit, and put it in the baking pan.

Let it rise until double. Bake it in the oven preheated to 425°F for about 12 minutes. Reduce the heat to 325°F and bake it one hour longer. Remove it from the oven, and as soon as it has lost some of the heat and it is possible to handle it, remove it from the pan, and peel off the wax paper. Return it to the turned off oven, placed on a cookie sheet, and leave it there for 12 hours to dry. *Panettone* should have a very dark, almost burned crust.

Wrap it in wax paper and keep it sealed in a cool place. It is best to refrigerate it if kept longer than one week.

It is very good served with tea, hot chocolate, or cappuccino. In Sicily *panettone* is cut in layers, like a cake, and spread with ricotta cream (see recipe, page 243).

This can be served in small pieces along with another Christmas dessert, like *Cucciddato*, page 273.

Note:

You could make 2 smaller loaves, adjusting the baking and drying times.

TORTA GELATO

Ice Cream Cake

Yield: 8 to 10 servings

Ice cream: ½ gallon vanilla in a rectangular container. You can
use ice milk instead. You can substitute for ¼ gallon vanilla,
¼ gallon chocolate, coffee, or strawberry
Cream: 1 cup, heavy, whipped very stiff (see Cream, page 41)
Cake: 4 to 5 layers Yellow Cake, page 249, baked in a 9- by 5- by
3-inch pan; or any other yellow or pound cake
Citron: 4 tablespoons, candied, in very small pieces
Chocolate: 2 ounces, semisweet, in very small pieces
Walnuts: 2 tablespoons, crushed
Rum: light

Line a rectangular loaf pan, 9- by 5- by 3-inches, with very
heavy freezer wrap or a layer of foil covered by a layer of wax
paper. Let plenty of paper overlap the pan edges. Chill.

Mix the whipped cream with 3 tablespoons of chocolate and 4
tablespoons citron. Chill. Unwrap the ice cream, cut one 1-inch
slice from the widest side; place it on the bottom of the pan over
the paper lining, pressing down so that the entire bottom is
covered. Add more, if necessary, to fill gaps. Spread one half of
the cream mixture on next; cover with a cake slice, and fill in
gaps with other cake cuttings. Sprinkle some rum over the cake.
Cover with another layer of ice cream; spread on it the remaining cream mixture. Cover with a cake layer, sprinkle with rum,
and add another layer of ice cream. Cover with the overlapping
paper. Place in the freezer for at least 4 hours.

Mix together the remaining chocolate and the walnuts; remove the cake from the pan, pulling it out from the overlapping lining. Turn on serving plate and peel off the lining. Pat walnut-chocolate mix on top and sides of the cake. Serve immediately or return to freezer until ready to serve.

CASSATA SICILIANA

Sicilian Easter Cake

Yield: 16 servings

Cake: 3 layers of Yellow Cake, see recipe page 249. About 10 inches in diameter and ½-inch thick
Filling: 3 pounds Ricotta Cream, see recipe page 243
Decoration: Pistachio Marzipan, see recipe page 290. And candied and glazed fruit, such as green and red cherries, kumquats, orange slices, apricots, and honey-dipped papaya

Liquid to moisten and flavor cake:
Orange juice: ¼ cup
Rum: ¼ cup, white; or you may use vodka
Note:
Before adding citron and chocolate to the ricotta cream, put aside 1½ cups of it. Instead of pistachio marzipan, you may use Almond Marzipan, page 291.

Place a layer of cake on a platter. Sprinkle some of the orange juice and rum on it. Cover with a generous layer of ricotta cream. Repeat layering cake and ricotta. To cover the last layer of cake, use the ricotta cream put aside.

With a knife shave off the cake all around the top, so that the sides of it will be slanted (the top diameter slightly smaller than the base). Cover the sides with the ricotta cream, smoothing it with a large knife blade.

Gather the marzipan in a block and slice it in five sections. Roll out each section between two sheets of wax paper until almost ⅛-inch thick. Peel off the wax paper from the top, turn the wax paper with the marzipan upside down, and peel off the other sheet of paper. The marzipan sections have to cover the sides of the cake. Trim the marzipan and fit the sections around the sides, matching the marzipan top edge with that of the cake. Let the extra, if any, overhang at the base; trim with a sharp knife. Pat the sections on the side to adhere smoothly.

Slice the papaya in thin ribbons; arrange them on the cake as outlining petals of a flower as large as the cake top. Place the largest of your fruit in the center or arrange several small ones together. Display the fruit on the cake very symmetrically—the design of it should look very distinct.

Cassata can be kept in the refrigerator for several days.

Note:

You can use some shortcuts to make cassata.

The marzipan making and rolling can be time consuming and frustrating. Instead of covering the sides of the cassata with marzipan, set aside 1¾ cups of ricotta cream before mixing in the citron and the chocolate.

Reserve 1½ cups of it for covering the top of the cake. Make into a paste ¾ cup pistachio (raw unsalted and blanched). Blend it with one quarter cup ricotta cream. Cover the sides of the *cassata* with this ricotta-cream-pistachio-paste mixture.

Assemble and decorate the cake the same way.

TORTA DI CRÊPES

Crêpes Torte

Yield: 12 servings

Batter:
Baking powder: ½ teaspoon
Flour: 1¼ cup, unbleached, all-purpose
Eggs: 2, extra-large
Milk: 1¼ cups
Cream: ¼ to ⅓ cup, heavy; add larger quantity of cream for lighter batter
Sugar: 1 to 3 teaspoons. Add the least quantity of sugar for salty filling
Salt: ½ teaspoon
Vanilla: ½ teaspoon

Glaze:
Apricot Glaze: 3 times the quantity; (see recipe page 252). Use only with milk and egg pudding filling

Filling:
Milk and Egg Pudding: double the quantity; (see recipe page 239) *or* Chocolate Pudding, double the quantity; (see recipe page 236)

Topping:
Cream: some, heavy, whipped till very stiff; (see Cream, page 41)

To make the batter:
Mix the dry ingredients in a bowl; add some milk; mix into a smooth paste. Add remaining milk in small amounts, thinning

the paste. Add ¼ cup cream, eggs, and vanilla; beat by hand until smooth or with electric beater on medium speed about 1 minute.

Cook in 10-inch heavy skillet, lightly greased with butter, over medium heat. Spoon in just enough batter to coat the bottom of the skillet, moving the skillet with a sweeping motion. When the edges start curling up turn the crêpe over and cook very briefly on the other side. Remove from the pan and fold it in half, keeping the side cooked first inside.

Assembling:
Stack up layers of crêpes, with or without glaze, covered with a layer of filling on a large plate. Offset the crêpe layers to make a mound with a base larger than the individual crêpes. Top with cream. Serve immediately.

Other Suggestions:
You may fill the crêpes mixed without vanilla with Ham Filling, page 136; Chicken Liver Filling, page 136; Beef or White Chicken Filling, page 137; and roll and bake them in a buttered dish at 375°F about thirty minutes. Use as first course.

CROCCANTE DI MERINGA E NOCI

Meringue and Walnut Crunch

Yield: 14 servings

Egg white: 1 cup at room temperature (make sure no particles
    of yolk are present)
Cream of tartar: ½ teaspoon
Sugar: 1 cup granulated; ½ cup confectioners'
Salt: a pinch

Walnuts: 2 cups, coarsely ground (measure 2 cups of walnut halves, grind after measuring)

Have ready three rectangles of parchment paper approximately 10 by 12 inches on cookie sheets. Preheat oven to 250°F.

Mix the granulated sugar, confectioners' sugar, and salt. Beat at medium speed of an electric hand beater or speed 6 of a Kitchen Aid mixer the egg white and the cream of tartar until it forms foamy bubbles. Add the sugar mixture in a thin stream,. Scrape the bowl a few times. By the time you have run out of sugar, the meringue will be almost ready; it should look shiny and smooth. Beat 1 more minute. The consistency should be such that if you pick up a small amount with a spoon it will hang down in a stiff peak. At this point you can fold in the walnuts.

Divide the meringue among the 3 parchment rectangles; spread it evenly, with a large knife blade, to about 1 inch short of the paper edge. Place in the oven. Ideally, you should bake the meringue using only one oven shelf. If you have a single oven, most likely it won't be large enough to accommodate the three rectangles on one shelf and you'll have to use both oven shelves. The heat distribution will affect the baking process. To get the 3 layers baked as evenly as possible, switch them after 1 hour of baking and repeat 3 more times at intervals of 30 minutes. Bake the meringue a total of 3 hours. Turn off the heat and leave in the oven, with closed doors, 3 more hours. Remove from oven. Place one hand, spread open, over the meringue; pick up the edge of the parchment with your other hand, and turn the layer down on the cookie sheet; peel off the parchment. Handle the meringue very gently or it will crumble. Don't hold it from the edges—to move it around insert your open hand under it, lifting it first with a large spatula.

Let it cool off. If you are not going to use it immediately, seal each layer individually in foil and store it in a very dry place or in the refrigerator.

Meringue can be very temperamental. Excessive moisture in

the air can damage it: while you are mixing it, baking it, and after it has been baked. Too many or too little walnuts may also be a source of trouble—the baking time gets affected. You want to come out with a *croccante*; that means crunchy and brittle and, as we are dealing with meringue, light. No matter how much humidity in the air or error in measuring the walnuts, you can bring it to that stage.

If after 3 hours of baking the edges feel slightly gummy bake a little longer, until, spot checking, you find the edges have dried out.

Don't forget that after it has cooled off it will absorb moisture and lose its brittleness.

Note:

Ways of using your croccante:

Spread and stack the layers with unsweetened whipped cream (see Cream, page 41; you may add semisweet chocolate shavings to the cream). Serve immediately. To keep, store in the freezer. These may be served right out of the freezer.

or

Spread the two bottom layers with *Crema Moka* (page 243), or *Crema al Burro e Cioccolato* (page 244); keep two heaping tablespoons to decorate the top layer. Refrigerate at least one hour before serving. Serve with whipped cream on the side. You can also freeze and serve right out of the freezer.

PASTA SFOGLIA CON PANNA E FRAGOLE

Puff Pastry with Cream and Strawberries

Yield: 16 servings

Pastry:
Flour: ½ pound, unbleached, all-purpose
Water: ⅔ cup, cold
Butter: ½ pound, unsalted; use the conventional 4 ounce butter
    sticks: split them in one half, lengthwise, while cold. Leave
    them on the counter until they start softening. Line them up
    very closely, to form an even layer, about 4½ by 5 inches.
    Put in the refrigerator
Patience: blended with a good deal of gentleness
Perseverance: if you don't succeed the first time

Filling:
Cream: 3 cups, heavy, whipped until very stiff (see Cream,
    page 41)
Sugar: ¼ cup confectioners'
Jam: 4 tablespoons, strawberry
Strawberries: 4 cups; cut off the red outer layer, discard the
    white spongy interior. Cut the red part in small pieces

Glaze:
Strawberry glaze: double the amount in recipe (page 252)

Do not try to make pasta *sfoglia* in warm weather—your chances
of success would be slim. The ideal room temperature in which
to make pasta *sfoglia* is between 65°F and 70°F. It would also be
helpful to work on a marble surface.
    Knead the flour and enough water to obtain a very smooth,
pliable dough. Dust it with flour, wrap it with wax paper, and
keep it in a cool place for 15 mintues. Take the butter out of the

refrigerator and let it sit on the counter while your dough is resting. Dust your working surface with flour.

Roll the dough in a rectangle about 6 by 12 inches. Place the butter, that should be cool but not refrigerator stiff, on the bottom half of the dough rectangle, from its center down to about ¾ inch away from the edges.

Double up the dough over the butter so that the edges of the two halves coincide; press the edges together all around to seal the butter in. Keeping the dough fold away from you, start rolling a dough rectangle to about 6 by 12 inches. Keep the rolling pin lightly dusted with flour and do the same with the surface you are working on. Roll with light motions; don't make a continuous rolling motion but make brief and repeated ones.

Roll the dough, always keeping one of the short sides toward you. You may turn it, inverting the surface sides up and down while you are rolling. As soon as you reach the 6- by 12-inch size, fold the dough in three, lengthwise, having the three sections overlap as accurately as possible.

Turn the dough so that the short side faces you and repeat the rolling procedure to obtain a 12- by 6-inch rectangle.

Fold it in 3 as before, wrap it in wax paper, and let it rest in a cool place for 15 minutes.

*Take the folded dough, short side toward you, roll it to 6 by 12 inches. Fold it; roll it out again; fold it; wrap it; let it rest 15 minutes.

Repeat from * and let the dough rest for 30 minutes.

After the 30 minute resting period you are ready to roll the dough out to be baked.

Preheat your oven to 450°F.

You should be able to roll out a dough layer about 11 by 22 inches wide and one-fifth-inch thick. The sides of this layer have to be trimmed to free the pastry layers and enable them to puff.

Cut a ½-inch strip all around and reserve it. Cut the strip in

2-inch sections—it makes good snack sticks. Use a very sharp pastry wheel.

Divide the dough in half, cutting through it with the pastry wheel, and you'll have 2 puff pastry layers, roughly 10 by 10 inches. Large pastry layers do not puff as much as small ones. You can cut individual pastries; out of each square you should get 10, 2 by 5 inches.

Lay the dough on cookie sheets. Bake it at 450°F for 10 minutes. Reduce the temperature to 375°F and bake the individual pastries 10 more minutes, the large squares 25 more minutes. Cuttings from trimming the dough will require only 5 more minutes. Let the puff pastry cool. Puff pastry, after it cools off, can be stored for a few days, well sealed in foil.

Beat the cream until stiff. Add 4 tablespoons strawberry jam; beat some more. The individual pastries can be cut in one half: the lower half brushed with glaze, filled with cream and strawberries; the upper half placed on top and dusted with confectioners' sugar.

The 2 large pastry squares may have puffed irregularly and because of the size, it might be hard to remove the top layer. Try to remove it if well detached from the lower part, cutting it with a long knife blade. Glaze, fill, and top like the small pastry. Each square will serve 8.

If the way the pastry has puffed makes it impossible to remove the top layer brush the glaze on top and cover with cream and strawberries. You may add the glaze sometime before serving the dessert; the cream and strawberries must be added just before serving. Serve dusted with confectioners' sugar.

Once you get the hang of it, you can work at making a single large pastry shell with sides. Cut 1-inch strips, lay them on the moistened edge of the larger layer, press them down gently, and score the pastry layer along the inside edge of the strip. You may use it as a first course using any filling recipe or pasta sauce recipe that you think might work.

CROCCANTE DI BIGNE' ALLA PANNA

Beignets Crunch

Yield: 12 servings

Dough for beignets:
Flour: 1¾ cups, unbleached, all-purpose
Butter: ¼ pound, unsalted
Eggs: 6, extra-large
Water: 1¼ cup
Sugar: 1 tablespoon
Salt: 1 pinch

Cream Filling:
Cream: 3 cups, heavy (see Cream, page 41)
Sugar: ¾ cup

Caramel topping:
Sugar: 1 cup
Water: 6 tablespoons

To make the beignets mix the flour with the sugar and the salt. Put the water in a heavy saucepan and bring it to a boil. Add the butter, swirling it around until it melts.

Add the flour mixture all at one time and stir very energetically over low heat, pushing the dough against the sides of the pan until it comes off them clean and gathers together in a ball, about three minutes. Remove the pan from the heat and stir the dough a few more times.

To beat the eggs in, you may use an electric mixer or do it by hand. By hand, add the eggs one by one, beating well, about 5 minutes, after each addition. The dough should look stringy and very elastic when ready. With the electric mixer, the process is faster. Add the eggs, 1 by 1, beating after each addition about 30 seconds. Use the lowest as each egg is added, then increase speed to medium. After you have added the last egg, beat the dough a few more minutes. When ready it should be very elastic and stringy from the beater to the sides of the bowl. Scrape the bowl and the beater a couple of times during the beating process. (In my Kitchen Aid mixer, I use the flat beater, and speeds 1 and 4.)

Drop the dough by the heaping teaspoonful on cookie sheets, best if lined with parchment, leaving a 1½- to 2-inch space between them.

Bake in oven preheated to 425°F for 8 minutes, or until puffy and their tops crack slightly. Reduce the heat to 350°F and bake 20 to 25 more minutes, until light golden in color.

Leave the beignets in the turned off oven for 30 minutes; finish cooling them away from drafts. Cut them in half, leaving them attached by part of one side. Beignets can be made a few days in advance and stored, well sealed, in the refrigerator. Before using them, heat them for 5 minutes in a 350°F oven to regain crispness.

To make the filling, beat the cream in a cold bowl until it reaches a light stage. Start adding the sugar in a stream, and beat until very stiff. Beat the cream just before you fill the beignets and when you are ready to assemble the dessert.

To make the caramel topping, boil the water and the sugar in a heavy saucepan over medium-low heat, stirring slowly, to get a clear honey-colored caramel. Remember that stirring fast can cause your caramel to "freeze" and crystallize. Make the caramel topping as soon as all the beignets have been filled with cream. Have one third of the beignets arranged in a round layer, on a serving plate with the rest of the beignets laid out close by. To assemble the beignets you have to be fast. Pour some of the hot caramel on the layer arranged on the plate, return the pan with the caramel to the burner, set very low.

Add another layer of beignets, smaller than the bottom ones. Pour caramel on top; set the caramel pan back on the burner; build a third layer of beignets, smaller than the second. Continue adding beignets and caramel until you have run out of them and formed a pyramid.

The assembled dessert can be refrigerated for a couple of hours before serving.

PASTA FROLLA

Pie Crust

Yield: enough for a single-crust 10-inch round pie or 8- by 11-inch rectangular

Flour: ½ pound, unbleached, all-purpose
Margarine: 7 tablespoons, unsalted at room temperature; or butter
Egg: 1, extra-large, room temperature
Sugar: 6 tablespoons
Salt: ½ teaspoon

Optional:
Lemon rind: ¼ teaspoon, grated

To mix, handle, and roll the crust see Rustic Pizza crust, page 139.

CROSTATA DI FRUTTA

Fruit Pie

Yield: 6 servings

Crust:
Pie crust: Use same quantity as called for in recipe (page 268)

Filling:
Apples: 5, large, peeled, quartered, cored; slice the quarters in
   ¹/₅-inch slices, holding each piece of apple so that the slices
   stay together. When ready to lay on the crust, push and
   press on the slices so that they are overlapping. You may
   use pears instead of apples
Sugar: 6 to 8 tablespoons
or
Instead of sugar, for a richer taste, use: apricot preserve, or
   marmalade: ½ to ¾ cup

Grease a pie pan well and dust with flour. I like to use a
rectangular pan, 8 by 11 inches.

Line it with the crust, reserving some strips for the lattice.

Arrange the fruit on the crust well below the top. Sprinkle the
sugar over the fruit, and crisscross the reserved strips on top.
Push down the edge of the crust to cover the ends of the lattice.

If you want to use the preserve or the marmalade, smooth a
layer of it on the crust bottom before adding the fruit; dab the
fruit top with what is left. Arrange the lattice.

Bake in oven preheated to 375°F for 40 to 50 minutes.

This pie can be unmolded without much chance of being left
with crumbs instead of a crust.

Let it cool awhile. When still slightly warm, run a knife all
around the edge to make sure no overboiled filling is going to

keep it stuck. Put a cookie sheet on top of it, turn it upside down, put another cookie sheet over the pie bottom, and turn it again, lattice side up. Slide on the serving plate.

Serve cold.

CROSTATA DI CREMA GIALLA

Milk-and-Egg Pudding Pie

Yield: 6 servings

Crust:
Pie crust: Use same quantity as called for in recipe (page 268)

Glaze:
Apricot or Orange: Same quantity as called for in recipe (page 252)

Filling:
Milk and egg pudding: 3 cups, lukewarm (see recipe, page 239)
Peaches: 6 halves, canned in syrup

Line an ungreased pie pan with crust 10-inch round, or a different shape of equal area, and prick the bottom and the sides well around.

Bake it in an oven preheated to 400°F for 10 to 20 minutes. Let it cool off, unmold, and put on the serving dish.

Brush the inside of the crust with the hot glaze, and arrange the peaches in it symmetrically, cut side down.

Pour the milk and egg pudding in, letting the rounded parts of the peaches surface.

Chill for 1 to 2 hours before serving.

CROSTATA MONTE BIANCO

Chestnut Pie

Yield: 8 servings

Crust:
Pie crust: Use same quantity as called for in recipe (page 268)

Filling:
Chestnut puree: 1, 250 gram can of *crème de marrons*, available in good food markets. Get the kind packed for dessert that is creamier and sweeter than the pureed chestnuts packed for generic cooking
Chestnuts: 20, packed in water; keep 8 whole, mash the rest coarsely
Cream: 1½ cups, heavy; (see Cream, page 41)
Cocoa: powder

Roll out the crust dough in two rectangles, equal in size, about 7½ by 9 inches each. Lay them on a cookie sheet. Prick the surfaces of both. With a long knife blade, make indentations on the top of one layer so that it is divided in 8 rectangles. Do not cut the dough all the way down to the cookie sheet.

Bake in oven preheated to 400°F about 10 to 12 minutes. Let the dough cool.

In the meantime prepare the filling. Whip the cream until very stiff. Set one quarter of it aside. Fold the *crème de marrons* with the larger quantity of cream; mix in the mashed chestnuts.

Cover the unscored layer of crust with the cream filling. Detach very gently the sections of dough of the other layer and lay them in the same order as they were on the filling. Press them down lightly until some filling oozes up between the sections. Put a little mound of the reserved cream on the middle of each section and place a chestnut on it.

Sift cocoa powder over the dessert; chill. The pie could be served immediately but it is best if served an hour or two after it has been assembled. The crust can be made in advance and stored well sealed in foil for a few days, taking care to keep the pieces of the scored layer in order.

CASSATA INFORNATA

Baked Cassata

Yield: 6 to 8 servings

Crust:
Pie crust: Use same quantity as called for in recipe (page 268)

Filling:
Ricotta cream: 3 cups (see recipe page 243)
Eggs: 2, extra-large
Vanilla: 1 teaspoon

Grease well and dust with flour a baking pan 10 inches round or any size equivalent in area. Choose one with sides 1½ inches high. Line it with dough, letting the dough overlap the edge of the pan slightly.

Mix the filling ingredients, stirring well by hand or at low speed with an electric mixer.

Fill the crust and fold the edges over the filling.

Bake in an oven preheated to 375°F for 30 minutes; reduce the heat to 300°F and bake it for 20 more minutes.

Serve cold.

"CUCCIDDATO"

Sicilian Christmas Dessert

Yield: served along with other Christmas desserts, this could serve up to 40 people; it is served in thin slices

Crust:

Flour: 2 ⅔ cups, unbleached, all-purpose

Margarine: 7 tablespoons, unsalted, room temperature; you may substitute one tablespoon of the margarine with one tablespoon of lard

Sugar: ⅓ cup

Salt: ½ teaspoon

Water: ½ cup, cold

Egg: 1, extra-large, separate yolk from white. Set aside both to finish the crust before baking it

Fig and raisin filling:

Raisins: 10 ounces, dark, seedless, half of them coarsely ground, half whole

Figs: 10 ounces, dry, finely ground

Papaya: 3 ounces, dry, honey-dipped, finely ground (available in many health food stores)

Citron: 1 ounce, finely cut in very small pieces

Walnuts: ½ pound; weigh shelled; finely ground

Honey: ¼ cup

Sugar: ⅓ cup

Cocoa: 2 tablespoons, powder

Rum: ¼ cup, light

Almond filling:
Almonds: 1 pound, blanched, finely ground
Papaya: 6½ ounces, honey-dipped, finely ground; (available in health food stores)
Water: 2 cups
Sugar: ¾ cup

Decoration:
Sugar: confectioners' mixed with some water
Glaze: (see recipe, page 252); use orange marmalade, the same quantity as called for in recipe
Pistachios: some, raw, unsalted, shelled, blanched, ground not too finely
Almonds: blanched
Walnuts: in halves
Cherries: candied

To make the crust:
Mix the dry ingredients and cut in the shortening, blending it into the dry ingredients until the mixture looks like coarse crumbs. Gather it together, make a well in the middle of it, and put the water in. Knead together until the dough is very smooth; add more water if necessary. Wrap it in wax paper and set it aside.

To make the fig and raisin filling:
Dissolve the sugar in the rum over low heat; mix all the ingredients together.

To assemble the fig and raisin cucciddato:
Take a little over one-half of the dough and roll it out in a 14-inch circle. Arrange the filling in a ring, packing it well together, leaving a 2½-inch space in the middle and a 3-inch space all around (measurements are a close approximation). Fold the dough over the filling, pinch the extra dough together at even intervals; you'll have about 8 folds of extra dough. Cut the extra, leaving enough to be able to pinch the ends together; set the

cuttings aside. Cut a cross in the center of the dough; lift the dough flaps up to meet the rest of the dough covering the filling. To patch a few uncovered places of filling, use the cuttings set aside. Ease the *cucciddato* on a cookie sheet. Rub with egg white all the places the crust has been joined; keep it from running to the bottom or it will make it stick. Brush the top with the egg yolk.

Make three rows of 1-inch slits across and all around the top, the two outer rows going down the sides a little bit.

To make the almond filling:
Cook the water and the sugar over low heat until reduced to a little less than half the volume. Stir occasionally. Add the almonds, mix them in well with the syrup, and cook, stirring, for a few minutes. Remove from the heat and mix well with the papaya.

To assemble the almond cucciddato:
Take a little less than half of the crust dough and roll it in an oval shape. Pack together the filling along the center of the longest diameter of the oval, tapering the filling toward the ends.

Lift the sides of the crust and let the edges come together right on top of the filling. Press them together to form a ½-inch ridge, brush with egg white, and then flute. Ease it on a cookie sheet. Make holes with a fork all along the top of the *cucciddato*. Traditionally the almond *cucciddato* has to have a very light color, so do not brush the top with egg yolk.

To bake both *cucciddati* have the oven preheated to 325°F. Bake between 1 hour and 1 hour and 15 minutes. If the fig *cucciddato* crust looks too pale, bake it a little longer.

To decorate the fig cucciddato *in the traditional way:*
Brush the top with hot glaze and sprinkle it with the pistachios. This could be done while the *cucciddato* is still hot or after it has cooled off. If you find the pistachio topping time consuming, stir some confectioners' sugar into water to make a thick paste.

Spread small quantities of it on top of the *cucciddato* and place candied cherries and walnuts on it.

To decorate the almond cucciddato *in the traditional way:*
Mix confectioners' sugar and water to the right consistency, and spread on top of the *cucciddato;* sprinkle it with pistachios. As in the fig *cucciddato* decoration, you might find the pistachio search and preparation time consuming. A nice alternative to it is to mix the sugar paste a little thicker and use it to stick almonds on in any arrangement that pleases your eye.

Cucciddati, well wrapped and unrefrigerated, will last easily a month without losing any of their qualities. After a month I would put any left over *cucciddato* in the refrigerator, though people in Sicily keep them in tins through the winter.

Cucciddati do not necessarily have to be large. They can be made in very small shapes and obviously baked a shorter time. If you do not feel like assembling the fig *cucciddato* in ring shape, you can make it in a loaflike shape, as some bakers do in Palermo.

PIGNOCCATA

Egg Dough and Honey Pastry

Yield: 8 servings

Flour: ½ pound, unbleached, all-purpose
Eggs: 2, extra-large, plus 1 egg yolk
Honey: ⅓ cup
Pistachio: 1 tablespoon, unsalted, shelled, ground not too finely
Oil: corn or made from seeds, enough to deep fry

Set aside ¼ cup flour. Make a well in the middle of the rest of the flour. Put in it the 2 whole eggs and the yolk, beat them with a fork, and start working the flour into the eggs. Knead to obtain a very smooth dough; add the flour set aside if the dough is too sticky. Shape the dough in a roll, 1½ inch thick, and cut it into 1-inch sections.

Roll out the sections to look like thin bread sticks ½-inch thick. Dust them well with flour. To better handle the dough work on a surface dusted with flour if your dough is soft, and moisten your hands if your dough is hard.

Line up a few of the rolls, dust them with flour again, and cut across them into nuggets about ½-inch long. Toss them lightly in flour to prevent them from sticking.

Heat the oil (not to the smoking point) and add enough nuggets to float freely; keep heat on medium to medium-high. The dough nuggets will swell to double the volume; remove them when they have acquired a golden color. Before adding another batch of nuggets, turn off heat for a couple of minutes; the dough will not cook properly if immersed in very hot oil. When you are finished frying the dough, warm up the honey in a skillet, on medium heat, until it looks runny. Add the fried dough bits and stir over low heat until they start sticking together. As soon as the honey caramellizes, remove from heat. Have a surface like a Formica counter top or a narble top lightly oiled. Drop the nuggets by the heaping spoonful on the oiled surface, making 8 mounds. Sprinkle the pistachio over them, let them cool for 5 minutes. Pack the nuggets with greased hands to give the mound a regular shape. Let the *pignoccata* cool completely before removing it from the oiled surface. Remove it gently, using a wide knife blade to detach it. *Pignoccata* is best eaten freshly made. In cool weather *pignoccata* will keep, wrapped loosely in wax paper, for a few days. In warmer weather it needs refrigeration.

BRIOSCINE

Small Brioches

Yield: 6 servings

Flour: 2¼ cups, unbleached, all-purpose
Yeast: 1 tablespoon, dry at room temperature
Egg yolks: 2, room temperature
Salt: ½ teaspoon
Sugar: 1 teaspoon
Water: 3 tablespoons, tepid
Milk: ½ cup

Filling:
Cream: 1 cup, heavy
Sugar: ¼ cup
and/or
Ice cream: your favorite

Dissolve yeast in some tepid water. Add the sugar. Add and knead in it ¼ cup of the flour, or enough to make a soft dough. Gather it into a ball. Place in a floured container and let it rise covered in a warm place until double in bulk. Mix the remaining flour with the salt, then knead it with the egg yolks and the milk. Add it to the yeast dough and knead together until well blended. To mix use the dough hook on an electric mixer (speed 2 and 4 of the Kitchen Aid), or knead by hand, and add more milk if necessary to make a soft, but not sticky, dough.

Let dough rise in a warm place until doubled. Beat it down. Shape 6 small brioches, place them on a baking sheet. Let brioches rise to about twice their size. Bake for 10 minutes in preheated 375°F oven; reduce to 325°F; brush the top with butter or with one egg yolk mixed with 1 tablespoon water; bake 10 more minutes.

Let them cool off.

Whip the cream until light, add the sugar, keep beating until very stiff; (see Cream, page 41). Cut the brioches in half—not quite through—and stuff them with the cream or the the ice cream or both.

"CASSATEDDE"

Ricotta-Cream-Filled Pastry

Yield: 10 to 11 servings

Crust:
Flour: 1¼ cups, unbleached, all-purpose
Margarine: 1 tablespoon, scant, unsalted, room temperature
Egg: 1, extra-large; separate the yolk from the white. Put the white in a small bowl.
Sugar: ½ tablespoon
Salt: a pinch
Water: a few tablespoons, up to 5 or 6
Oil: corn or made from seeds, enough to deep fry

Filling:
Ricotta cream: 1 cup (see recipe, page 243); use the least amount of sugar suggested and add a little extra chocolate. Be extra fastidious in draining the excess liquid of the ricotta

Topping:
Sugar: confectioners'

Mix the dry ingredients with the margarine and the egg yolk; start adding the water, a tablespoon at a time. Knead to obtain a stiff dough. Divide the dough in 4 pieces, roll each piece out in a strip approximately 4 by 9 inches; (to knead and roll out the dough see *Pasta di Semola*, page 83). Cut it across so that you have two 4 by 4½-inch pieces of dough. Place a tablespoon of ricotta cream in the middle of each one. Pick up one of the shortest sides of the dough and fold it over the filling; with a pastry wheel round up the corners so that you get a half-moon shape. Put the cuttings aside.

Pick up the *cassatedde* and pinch the edges together to seal them; you should pinch close to ½ inch of the dough edge. Lay the *cassatedde* on a floured surface and cover them.

Repeat until you run out of dough. From the cuttings you should be able to make 2 or 3 more *cassatedde*.

Have enough oil in a deep fryer to let the pastry float freely. Warm it (not to the smoking point). Have heat on medium.

Holding the pastry from the middle, dip the sealed edges in the egg white, and then put it in the oil. Turn the *cassatedde* often; they should be ready to be taken out of the oil in about 3 minutes. Lay them in a paper towel-lined dish.

Cassatedde are eaten hot sprinkled with confectioners' sugar. They can be made in advance, warmed up for a few minutes in the oven, preheated at 350°F, and sprinkled with sugar just before serving. I personally like to eat them as they have reached room temperature without the sugar topping.

Note:

To cut the pastry crust I use a zigzag-edged pastry wheel, which is used also to cut and seal ravioli and any filled pastry.

CANNOLI

A Ricotta-filled Pastry

Yield: 60 to 65 shells, 4 inches long

Crust:
Flour: 3 ¾ cups, unbleached, all-purpose
Margarine: 3½ tablespoons, unsalted
Sugar: 3 tablespoons
Eggs: 2, extra large; separate the yolk and the white of one. Put
    the white in a small bowl. Set aside
Lemon: ½, juice only
Wine: ¼ cup, dry, red
Water: 6 to 8 tablespoons
Oil: corn or made from seeds, enough to deep fry

To make the cannoli *shells you'll need:*
Some aluminum *cannoli* tubes: they are easily found in kitchen
    supplies' stores, get 4 to 12
A manual pasta machine: Atlas mod. 150 lusso, to roll out the
    dough; any mention of settings has to be referred to this
    machine
Tongs: to get a good grip of the aluminum *cannoli* tubes

Filling:
Enough to fill about 10 shells
Ricotta cream: 1 pound (see recipe, page 243)

Topping:
Pistachio: some, raw, shelled, unsalted, not too finely ground
Orange peel: a few strips, candied (see Candied Orange Peel,
    page 291); or commercially available peel, candied, glazed,
    or packed in syrup
Sugar: confectioners'

The topping is not strictly necessary but it does add to the esthetics of the dessert, and it is a subtle addition to the taste. Using the orange peel and the sugar, and skipping the pistachio will be enough to enhance the dessert.

To make the shells:
By rubbing and squeezing the ingredients in your hands, mix the flour, sugar, margarine, one whole egg, and one yolk well.

Add the lemon juice, wine, and a few tablespoons of water.

Start kneading, adding small quantities of water, until you obtain a very stiff smooth dough. Gather the dough and divide it in 8 equal pieces. You are ready now to roll the dough. To do it by hand is very hard and time consuming. If you have a manual pasta machine, it is an easy operation. Read Rolling Out the Dough in the recipe *Pasta di Semola*, page 83.

After you have put your first strip of dough through setting number 4, by the fifth time you should have a strip that will yield 6 squares, 4 by 4 inches. Set the cuttings aside and keep them covered (as soon as you have collected all the trimmings of extra dough, knead them briefly together, and roll them to obtain more *cannoli* shells).

To cut the squares use a pastry wheel. I use one with a zigzag edge that is used also to cut and seal ravioli and any kind of filled pastry.

Trim the squares' corners to obtain rounds using the same wheel. Set the rounds aside while you are working with another strip of dough; after they have dried for a few minutes, put them through the pasta machine again (set on 4) three times. Control the way they stretch, turning them around to give them an oval shape.

Do not work with more than 12 rounds at a time. As soon as you have rolled the twelfth round into an oval shape you are ready to shape and fry the first shells. Heat a 2½-inch deep layer of oil in a vessel for deep frying, almost to the smoking point.

While the oil is heating, dip the empty *cannoli* tubes in it. Pull them out and set them to drain on a paper towel.

Place the *cannoli* tubes on the middle of the dough ovals along the shorter diameter. One end of the tubes should be lined up with the dough edge on one side and the other end overlap the dough edge on the other side.

Pick up one side of the dough oval and fold it over so that the tip of it lies on the top of the aluminum tube. Dab some of the reserved egg white on the tip of the dough oval that rests on the tube (making sure you don't let it run on the tube). Pick up the other side of the oval and fold it over the tube so that about ⅓ inch of the oval tips overlap. Firmly tap the overlapping tips to seal them (the egg white is indispensable to a good seal—without it your shell would open up). The dough should be very loose on the tube. As soon as you have at least 4 *cannoli* sealed on the tubes, reduce the heat to low, and test the oil by frying a scrap of dough. See how long it takes it to get a nice golden color. Adjust the heat to medium, and put the *cannoli* in the oil. For your first try you might want to start with just one. It should take the shell only a few seconds to get bubbly and start getting crisp. With the tongs, get a good grasp of the end of the tube that protrudes and slip the tube out pushing the shell at the same time with the tip of a cooking fork, being careful not to puncture it. If the tube offers resistance, do not worry; let it stay in the oil, the paler side turned down, and try frying another shell. When you succeed in slipping a tube out, let the shell cook longer, unless of course, you haven't got your timing or the heat well adjusted and the shell needs no further browning.

Do not ignore the first shell put in the oil. In a few seconds it will be hard enough for you to grasp the tube with the tongs and get hold of the shell with your hand through several pieces of paper towel doubled up together. Rotate the shell without squeezing it—that should detach it from the tube. Let it cook a little longer if necessary.

Once you get the hang of it you should be able to put 4 to 5 shells in the oil, one right after another. As soon as you have put the fourth or fifth shell in, the tube of the first shell put in the oil should be ready to be slipped out, followed immediately by the others. Once all the tubes are out, if your timing and your heat are right, the *cannoli* can fry a little longer before getting their typical rich golden color.

One thing to do immediately if the tubes stick is to reduce the heat to low giving yourself more time to act. And, as you wrap more dough ovals around the tubes, check the way you seal the tips together; stray egg white is often guilty for sticky shells.

Let the shells drain on a paper towel-covered dish. Choose one with sides high enough to be able to stand the shells against them to better let the excess oil run down.

The shells, well sealed in a tin container, lined with wax paper, will last for more than a month.

Fill the shells with cream from a pastry tube or stuff the cream in with a knife blade just before serving (no more than one hour before).

Sprinkle the pistachio on the ricotta at the ends and place on the center of each end a little bit of orange peel, cut in rounds, squares, or strips.

Dust the crust with confectioners' sugar.

Note:

Shells can also be frozen and used right out of the freezer.

SFINCE DI SAN GIUSEPPE

Saint Joseph Beignets

Yield: about 13 to 14 very large beignets

Flour: 1¾ cups, unbleached, all-purpose
Lard: ¼ pound
Water: 1¼ cup
Eggs: 6, extra-large
Oil: corn or made from seeds, 1 quart

Filling:
Ricotta cream: up to 5 pounds; (see recipe, page 243)

Boil water, add lard, and stir until dissolved. Add flour all at one time; stir over low heat until it gathers into a ball. Remove from heat. Let it cool.

Beat eggs completely, one at a time. If you are using a counter-top mixer use the speed suggested by the manufacturer for choux batter, or lowest speed initially, increasing to medium. Cover and refrigerate the dough for 1 hour. Keep in mind that when dough is fried, it expands to almost 3 times its volume, and that you will fry it by the very heaping spoonful. Choose a frying vessel that will let at least 3 float and expand uncrowded.

Heat oil as for deep frying; reduce heat to medium-low; add batter by the heaping spoonful. Batter should turn itself upside down; if it doesn't within 4 to 5 minutes, turn it and hit the *sfince* with the edge of a wooden spoon. As you see *sfince* pop, turn them so that the side that just popped is down in the oil; keep on doing this until the spoonful is about 3 times the uncooked volume. It will take approximately 15 minutes. Remove from oil; drain on paper towel. *Sfince* are best eaten fresh. To keep a few days, wrap in wax paper and put in a sealed container in a cool place. Before using them put them spread on a cookie sheet with sides, in a 450°F preheated oven, for about 5 minutes to crisp them.

Cool before filling.

PATATE

"Potatoes"

Yield: 12 "potatoes"

Cupcakes: 12, small; use the Yellow Cake recipe, page 249.
   Split the cup cakes in two layers

Filling:
Chocolate: 3 ounces, semisweet, melted in a double boiler
Kirsch: 1½ ounces; or use brandy, vodka, or white rum
Butter: 6 ounces, unsalted at room temperature
or, instead of the above filling, use:
Milk and Egg Pudding: about 1 cup, see recipe, page 240

Potato "peel":
Marzipan: 14 ounces, almond, page 291
Sugar: 1 ⅓ cup, confectioners'
Cocoa: 2 cups
Honey: a few teaspoons

Potato "eyes":
Pine nuts: a few

Have some liqueur, preferably the same used for the filling, to sprinkle on the cake.

Beat butter with electric beater at medium speed until light, 4 to 5 minutes. Beat in the melted chocolate and blend well.

Add the kirsch and beat one more minute. Put in the refrigerator until stiff enough to spread without running.

Knead together marzipan, sugar, ⅔ cup cocoa, and honey. You may mix it in the food processor, if you have one, but do not wait for the ingredients to gather into a dough ball, as overbeating and the heat that develops changes the consistency of the marzipan.

Take it out as soon as it looks grainy, like coarse cornmeal, and finish kneading by hand. The marzipan dough will be ready when, rolled in a cylinder on the counter, it looks smooth and shiny. If you are having trouble getting it to the right consistency it could be because it is too dry or too sticky. Add a few drops of honey if too dry, or a very small amount of sugar if too sticky. Roll in a 2-inch roll and seal in foil.

Sprinkle a good amount of kirsch on both halves of the cup cakes. Spread a layer of chocolate filling on the bottom halves or some milk and egg pudding. Place the top halves over them. Trim the very tip of the top edge of the cup cakes to give them an oval shape.

Divide the marzipan roll in 12 sections and roll them in rounds between two sheets of wax paper. Don't expect to get the right size layer (large enough to wrap the cup cake) at first roll. Roll out the marzipan and peel the top layer of wax paper but don't try to pull the marzipan from the bottom layer of paper. Rather turn it down on top of the wax paper you just peeled off and detach the paper gently.

Replace the wax paper on the marzipan, roll it out some more, and remove the wax paper as you did before. As long as you do a good peeling job, you'll turn out a perfect "peel." Always remove the wax paper before it creases too much, as it will be impossible to remove it without breaking the marzipan layer. Repeat until the marzipan layer is large enough to wrap around your cupcake.

To wrap the "potato peel" around your cupcakes hold a layer of marzipan on the palm of your hand, slightly cupped. Place the cupcake on it, rounded top down. Cup your hand a little more and mold it around. Gather the edge over the bottom of the cupcake to cover it entirely. Press the edge in little folds all around. If there is excess dough and this makes the bottom of the potato too bulky, remove the extra pieces.

Turn the bottom down on your cupped hand and mold the potato some more. Put the remaining cocoa on some wax paper. Roll the potato in it, then take it between your cupped hands and pat it.

Place it bottom down on a plate. Now you can add the "eyes." Poke the pine nuts into the potato, the thicker end down.

Serve them in a basket.

CORNETTI

Little Horns

Yield: 8 servings

Almonds: ⅔ cup, blanched, lightly toasted, ground coarsely; measure before grinding
Sugar: 2 cups
Water: ½ cup

Filling:
Cream: 1 cup, heavy, whipped till very stiff with no sugar (see Cream, page 41)
Strawberries: some, use only the outer layer, cut in very small pieces

Have a large piece of foil flat on the counter to accommodate

8 rounds, each 4 inches. The counter must not be marble.
Select and have ready a large spoon that will contain about ¼
cup liquid.

To prepare almonds place them on a cookie sheet in preheated 375°F oven for 7 to 10 minutes. Stir around a few times
while baking. Remove from oven as they barely turn color. Let
them cool off, grind, and return to the turned off oven.

Place sugar and water in a heavy 6-inch pan over medium-
high heat. Occasionally stir slowly. Mixture will turn syrupy
and caramelize in 10 to 15 mintues; the surface will look foamy.
As it turns to light caramel color (about 320°F—use a candy
thermometer) reduce to very low heat and stir slowly. As the
color darkens a bit, add almonds, and keep stirring slowly until
well mixed. From this point on work very quickly. Using the
large spoon, pour the mixture by the spoonful on the foil to form
rounds the size of a demitasse saucer, keeping some space between the rounds.

Starting with the first round, tear the foil encircling it; keep
track of the order you have been pouring the mixture. As all the
rounds are now in their own section of foil and as they have lost
enough heat so that they can be handled, shape them into cones
starting from the first poured and with the help of the foil. Work
quickly—as the caramel cools it cannot be molded. Shaping the
caramel rounds like *cannoli* shells will be easier when you are
familiar with handling the caramel.

In making *cornetti* use your common sense. If you see the heat
is burning the sugar too quickly, reduce it. If the sugar crystallizes, increase it. Also, remember that stirring fast (in addition to
removing the pan from the heat) will help cool off a caramel that
is getting burned. However, stirring a crystallized caramel
quickly will only crystallize it more.

It might be necessary to keep molding the *cornetti* in the cone
shape until they cool; as long as the caramel is warm, they
will slump. Putting the handle of a wooden spoon inside them
will help mold them. Kitchen specialty stores sometimes carry

tin or wood cone-shaped forms. They are hard to find but they work best.

Fill with the cream and cover the end with strawberry bits.

Note:

You may coat the edges of the *cornetti* with melted semi-sweet chocolate (see Chocolate Covered Candied Orange Peel, page 292).

PASTA REALE DI PISTACCHIO

Pistachio Marzipan

Pistachios: ¾ cup raw, unsalted, shelled, blanched
Almonds: ¾ cup, blanched
Sugar: ½ cup, confectioners'
Honey: up to 2 teaspoons

Make pistachios and almonds into a paste in the food processor. Knead in the sugar. Test and see if pliable enough to mold; if not, start adding small quantities of honey. If too soft add more sugar. As soon as you feel the paste can be handled without coming apart stop adding the honey or the sugar. Gather it into a ball. Wrap tightly in plastic until ready to use. You may stretch the marzipan by adding larger quantities of sugar and blending in enough honey to keep the paste pliable.

PASTA REALE DI MANDORLE

Almond Marzipan

Almond paste: 6 ounces, available in good supermarkets
Sugar: confectioners'
Food coloring (only for *cassata*): green, a few drops

Knead almond paste, adding small quantities of sugar until easy to handle. Some brandy of almond paste might need a little honey or corn syrup to be pliable enough to shape the desired way. You may stretch the marzipan, adding larger quantities of sugar and blending in enough honey to keep the paste pliable.

SCORZE D'ARANCIA CANDITE

Candied Orange Peel

Yield: 2 to 3 cups

Orange peel: 2 navel oranges; try to find oranges with thick peel. A few blemishes and discoloration on the peel won't hurt. Stand the oranges on stem ends. Cut through the peel vertically, dividing it into 6 or more sections. Cut and discard the 2 poles; detach the sections; try to leave all of the white part attached to peel. Soak in cold water 4 days. Change water and rinse well at least once every 24 hours. Cut in strips, a little wider than ⅓ of an inch or as narrow as ¼ of an inch
Sugar: 1 cup
Water: ½ cup

Place all the ingredients in a low-sided pan where the peel won't be too crowded (1-inch layer, more or less).

Cook over low heat at a low boil, uncovered, for about 20 minutes.

If liquid decreases too quickly, lower heat further, if possible, or cover. Increase heat to high; stir slowly at first; as liquid decreases and turns into a light syrup (about 5 minutes), stir more quickly. Syrup will get thicker and coat peel; strips will be sticking together. Move peel around very quickly, insert the spoon in between the peel, lift it slightly from the pan and turn it until you see that sugar has started caramelizing. Remove the pan from heat immediately and keep stirring the peel around until it crystallizes. Sugar will turn whitish and the spoon will make a rubbing noise as you stir. Finish cooling in the same pan, or for faster result, in a large dish. This keeps well in the refrigerator for a few weeks if wrapped in wax paper and sealed.

SCORZE D'ARANCIA CANDITE RICOPERTE DI CIOCCOLATA

Chocolate Covered Candied Orange Peel

Yield: 3 to 4 cups

Candied orange peel: see recipe, page 291, use quantity suggested in recipe
Chocolate: 4 ounces, semisweet, cut in small pieces

Cover a cookie sheet with wax paper. Put the chocolate in the top part of a double boiler. Set aside. Put some water in the bottom part of the double boiler, let it come to a boil, and reduce the heat to low. Place the top of the double boiler in the bottom part, cover it, and let it sit 15 minutes on low heat. Uncover it and stir the chocolate.

Coat only one half of each strip with chocolate. Holding it by one end; dip the other end in the chocolate. Bring up some chocolate with a flat wooden spoon and roll the orange peel on it until one half of it is well coated. Remove the excess by scraping it against the edge of the spoon. Lay the strips on the wax paper and chill them until the chocolate is well set. Wrap them in wax paper, seal them in a container, and refrigerate. This keeps for a few weeks.

Any chocolate left over can be kept in wax paper for further use. If you wish to coat the whole peel; wait until the chocolate covering the halves is set; warm up more chocolate in the meantime and coat the other half the same way as before.

BISCOTTINI ALLE NOCI

Walnut Cookies

Yield: 20

Flour: 6 ounces, unbleached, all-purpose
Walnuts: 1 cup
Butter: 6 tablespoons, unsalted, room temperature
Sugar: ½ cup
Egg yolk: 1
Salt: ¼ teaspoon

Optional:
Chocolate: 2 ounces, see Chocolate Covered Orange Peel; melt it the same way as in that recipe, page 292

If you have a food processor, blend all the ingredients in it until they gather into a ball. It will take a couple of minutes. If you do not have a food processor, mash the walnuts into a paste (use a mortar or a rolling pin).

Beat all the ingredients together with an electric beater until well blended.

Divide the dough into 20 equal parts. Roll each into a cylinder about 9 inches long, fold the ends to the center, and lay it on a cookie sheet. Leave a 1-inch space between the cookies.

If the walnuts have been ground by hand, the dough might not hold together well enough to roll as above; if so, pat it into a round shape.

Bake in oven preheated to 350°F for 15 to 20 minutes. When done, cookies will be very lightly colored on the top and the bottom will have turned light brown. Cool; use a spatula to remove them from the cookie sheet. If you wish to add a touch of chocolate to the cookies, melt the chocolate, fill a spoon with it (hold it over the double boiler) and quickly dip in it three parts of the curved edge of the cookie. Place them on a cookie sheet covered with wax paper. Chill and keep refrigerated, well sealed.

PASTINE ALLA NOCCIOLA

Hazelnut Pastry

Yield: about 20

Flour: 1 cup, unbleached, all-purpose
Butter: 7 tablespoons, unsalted
Brown sugar: ¼ cup
Egg: 1, extra-large, separate yolk from white
Hazelnuts: ¾ cup, ground

Salt: a pinch
Preserves: some, your favorite kind
Vanilla: 1 teaspoon

Melt the butter in a bowl placed in a pan with hot water; add the sugar and mix well. Mix the flour and the salt. Remove the bowl from the hot water. Beat the butter-sugar mixture, the yolk, and vanilla until smooth; beat in the flour until you obtain a dough without lumps.

Gather it, cover, and place in the refrigerator for 15 minutes.

Roll little balls the size of small walnuts, coat them with the egg white, and roll them in the hazelnuts.

Place on a cookie sheet with sides and bake them at 250°F in a preheated oven for about 10 minutes. Remove them from oven and make a small depression in the center of each cookie with the tip of a small spoon.

Add a small amount of preserve to fill the depression.

Return to oven and bake 40 more minutes.

NOCI E DATTERI IMBOTTITI

Stuffed Walnuts and Dates

Walnuts: some, shelled, in halves
Dates: some, pitted, cut along one side
Marzipan: some, see Pistachio Marzipan, page 290 and Almond Marzipan, page 291

You may also use:
Figs: dry, cut along one side

Ball up small amounts of marzipan and place it between the walnut halves, or in the split of the dates and the figs, leaving some of it exposed. Make indentations on the exposed marzipan with a knife blade in a diamond pattern.

Espresso making

To drink good espresso (not "expresso") you do not need any expensive machinery. All that is required is the top of the stove and a coffee pot for espresso. The pots come in several sizes, make coffee in a few minutes, and are easy to use. The pot is usually made of heavy aluminum and it works on a steam principle. The water is put in the bottom part of the pot up to the steam valve (the steam valve assures safe functioning). Then the filter is inserted and filled with coffee to the edge. The top part is screwed on, and the whole apparatus is placed on the burner on medium heat. The coffee will start coming up from the spout in the top part as soon as the water boils.

The most common trouble with coffee making is the coffee coming up too fast (therefore, too weak) or coming up too slowly (therefore getting too bitter and losing aroma by coming to a boil and standing too long in the upper part of the pot).

If either thing happens, something is wrong with the way the filter is loaded or with the way the coffee is ground. Underloading the filter and/or coarsely ground coffee will give you a weak coffee; overloading the filter and/or too finely ground coffee will cause the opposite problem.

Coffee for espresso should be ground a good deal finer than it is usually found in this country. The grind should be halfway between that of espresso and Turkish coffee.

In Italy espresso is served *without* lemon peel.

Suggestions
For Easy Menus

Pasta con l'Acciuga	114	Pasta with Anchovies
Saltimbocca	155	"Jump in the Mouth"
Broccolo Affogato	209	Braised Cauliflower with Olives
Pastine alla Nocciola	294	Hazelnut Pastry
Trenette agli "Sparacelli"	99	Trenette with Broccoli
Agnello al Forno	170	Roast Lamb
Patate al Forno	227	Baked Potatoes
Gelo di Melone	235	Watermelon Pudding
Margherite con Pomodoro e Ricotta	93	Margherite with Tomatoes and Ricotta
Scaloppine di Maiale al Vino	158	Pork Scaloppine in Wine
Patate alla Ghiotta	230	Glutton's Potatoes
Pere Infornate	234	Baked Pears
Minestra di Lenticchie	142	Lentil Soup
Uova al Pomodoro	183	Eggs in Tomato Sauce
Funghi Trifolati	206	Sauteed Mushrooms
Timballo all'Italiana	252	Italian Timbale
Conchiglie con Zucchine a "Tutto Dentro"	98	Pasta Shells with Braised Zucchini
Arrosto alla Palermitana	148	Palermo Roasted Beef Slices
Insalata di Spinaci	200	Spinach Salad
Bianco Mangiare	241	White Pudding
Pesto Trapanese	96	Pesto from Trapani
Filetti di Sogliola al Gratin	186	Sole Fillets, au gratin
Fagiolini Soffritti	205	Stir-fried String Beans
Crema al Caffè Chantilly	239	Coffee Pudding Chantilly

Note:

Fresh fruit can be freely substituted for all the desserts in the menus. Coffee (preferably espresso) should be served at the end of the meal.

INDEX